'A most engrossing narrative, with the author evidently enjoying nearly every minute of his wanderings'
The Sphere, 1952

In 1950, Anthony Rhodes announc[ed] travelling through the Sabine footh[ills] to Rome, on a donkey in the traditio[n of] Stevenson or Hilaire Belloc. To thi[s end] the villainous-looking, but very a[miable], Guiseppe Masceri and his unprepossessing donkey, Pepe.

Together they travelled south under the scorching sun, through lush valleys, mountain scrubs and distinctive villages, coming across all manner of odd characters on their way: from nuns and French commercial travellers to an international 'financier' and a man who had a strong liking for earthquakes!

'One of those imaginative yet learned travellers who deserve a special place in the history of English prose'
Peter Quennell

This new edition is introduced by Peter Quennell, editor of the *Memoirs of William Hickey* and *Mayhew's London Underworld*, both published in the Century Lives and Letters series.

ANTHONY RHODES

A
SABINE JOURNEY
To Rome in Holy Year

CENTURY
LONDON MELBOURNE AUCKLAND JOHANNESBURG

First published in 1952 by Putnam & Company

This edition first published in 1987 by Century, an imprint of Century Hutchinson Ltd, Brookmount House, 62–65 Chandos Place, London WC2N 4NW

Century Hutchinson Australia Pty Ltd
PO Box 496, 16–22 Church Street, Hawthorn, Victoria 3122, Australia

Century Hutchinson New Zealand Limited
PO Box 40–086, Glenfield, Auckland 10, New Zealand

Century Hutchinson South Africa (Pty) Ltd
PO Box 337, Berglvei, 2012 South Africa

ISBN 0 7126 1706 X

The publishers regret that they have been unable to reproduce the original photographs in this edition

Contents

TO
Peter Price

Introduction

Since 1625, when Samuel Purchas published the eccentric travelogue he called his *Pilgrimęs* – a book that pleased his contemporaries, though they sometimes refused to credit his more remarkable tales – the adventurous English Traveller has become a well-established literary type, which during the last century-and-a-half has produced such distinguished exponents as Borrow, Burton, Kinglake, Doughty and, in our own days, Norman Douglas, Rose Macaulay and the intrepid Freya Stark. Their range of interests has been extremely diverse; but each has drawn a vivid self-portrait; and, besides evoking the historical background and the imaginative atmosphere of the countries they have described, they have always been conscious of the human scene, and given us lively sketches of the strange characters they have met and talked with on the way.

To this group belongs the author of *A Sabine Journey*, who in 1950 set out on a leisurely jaunt from the mountains of Central Italy, a region of ancient towns and villages that often recalled the distant pre-Roman past, to celebrate the Catholic Holy Year. When his narrative opens, he is still standing at Terni, a little township close to the foot of the Sabine Mountains, and asking every peasant who enters with donkeys if he could hire one of their animals for a month, but receiving puzzled answers. 'It sounded perhaps rather an odd question ... Why couldn't I go to Rome anyway by bus?' The service, they declared, was excellent. His innkeeper echoed their surprise, even criticising the young Englishman's command of the Italian language, 'which,' he said, 'was clearly not good enough to serve me in these "savage parts"'.

At last, however, he hired a donkey named Pepe, who proved a calm and energetic beast, and its owner Giuseppe, whose ugly unshaven face, 'although a good deal of Italy was written on it, did not immediately prepossess me in his favour'; and one sunny May morning they began to climb.

The landscape they then penetrated was, if not savage, decidedly rough and wild, and has long been considered an unusually backward part of Italy. Among the ancient Romans, despite the fact that it was once the country home of their great Augustan poet Horace, it had already a slightly formidable reputation; and a Classical Dictionary informs us that its denizens, the Sabine people, had never, as a whole, 'acquired any high degree of civilization or mental culture ...'

And so it is today. The district is richly cultivated and frequently beautiful; but it is still unused to Northern visitors; and in one village, Fossa, between Aquila and Sulmona, the latter being a fairly sophisticated town, which has an hotel and three cinemas, Anthony Rhodes heard from a priestly pedagogue that he was 'the first foreigner they had had for four years'. The schoolboys were then granted a day's holiday, and ran off yelling with delight.

At this juncture it is probably worth noting that the Abruzzi, of which the vicinity of Sulmona is the richest and most fertile neighbourhood, has also been admirably portrayed by a modern English novelist. In *The Lost Girl* D. H. Lawrence sends his heroine Alvina to a lonely farmhouse there, and depicts 'the mountain foothills: irregular steep little hills half wild with twiggy brown oak-trees and marshes and broom heaths ... and the grand, pagan twilight of the valleys, savage, cold, with a sense of ancient gods who know the right for human sacrifice'.

On his journey Anthony Rhodes, too, finds many reminiscences of the country's pagan background; but, at the same time, he pictures the Middle Ages and writes expressively of feudal strongholds and monastic institutions – for example, the notorious Abbey of Subiaco, where 'the monks became train-band captains, levying war right and left in the Campagna', where 'the terrible Cenci matricide' that Shelley dramatised had taken place, the ferocious Colonna family long held their court, and the last Colonna Cardinal-Abbot is said to have lived with his mistress, Arthemise, 'who replaced him in charge of the Abbey whenever he was called away'.

Of all the tyrants, saints and hermits who populate Anthony Rhodes' story a single man of poetic genius stands forth; and here he is commemorated in an especially engaging chapter. The poet Horace, Quintus Horatius Flaccus, the Emperor Augustus' protégé, who was born in 65 BC, and died at the age of nearly fifty-seven, was presented about the year 34 AD by Augustus' cultivated minister Maecenas with the delightful Sabine farm at which he spent the remainder of his life, writing, entertaining his friends, picnicking, drinking good Falernian wine and repeatedly falling in and out of love.

This was the Golden Age of Latin verse; but, whereas some of his fellow versifiers, particularly Propertius and a close friend Tibullus, have been likened by Cyril Connolly in his essay on 'The Elegiac Temperament' to the 'poètes maudits' of the nineteenth century and led somewhat restless and disordered lives, Horace, notwithstanding one or two early setbacks (as when, on active service during the Civil Wars, he threw down his shield and fled at the Battle of Philippi) so far as we can judge from his own writing had a happy and harmonious career.

Only the foundations of his beloved farm remain. It consisted of some twenty rooms, built around a garden and two spacious courtyards, a *Nymphaeum*, or shrine of the Nymphs, which included a bathroom, and his bedroom, which had a fine mosaic pavement that the guide still points out. It stood in the valley of the Licenza and, Horace tells us, amid steep hills, slanting north and south; and his fields, which were warm and well-lit, bore olives, apples, vines and elms. His gardens were full of flowers and statues, overshadowed by clipped hedges of box and green bay, arranged in symmetrical patterns that suggest the gardening designs of the Renaissance.

From Horace's rustic paradise the author next moved on to his ultimate destination, Rome, and thus re-entered modern Italy. There the mood of the narration changes; but it loses none of its descriptive edge. In the Sacred City, which he both reveres and abhors, he encounters numerous odd representatives of the twentieth century Roman world, ranging from beggars, pimps and white-robed Abyssinians, selling patent medicines and drugs, to a rich American hostess, who patronised modern art of the more repulsive kind, and a Cardinal's private secretary, dressed in a black cassock and a silken skull cap, with a magnificent amethyst glittering on his finger.

Meanwhile Giuseppe and Pepe had both left him; evidently they missed their lonely mountain village. And Giuseppe, though he had never seen Rome before, was so unimpressed, even by the garish splendours of Ciampino airport, that, as soon as they had settled their accounts and he had drunk a single glass of wine, he announced that he proposed at once to ride home and doze through the night upon his donkey's back.

While Anthony Rhodes watched them 'lumping down the road together' towards the classic Milvian Bridge – the site of the Emperor Constantine's victory, beneath the Sign of the Cross, over his pagan adversary Maxentius – he himself was preparing to celebrate the triumph of the Christian faith in Bernini's majestic square before St Peter's. This celebration completed his journey. It had been a journey well worth making, which he describes with sympathy and skill. He has a trained historical sense, accompanied by a keen appreciation of Nature and the works of man, and, as this book shows, is one of those imaginative yet learned travellers who deserve, I think, a special place in the history of English prose.

Peter Quennell
1987

CHAPTER ONE

The Sabine Mountains

THE SABINE MOUNTAINS run parallel with the Apennines, to which they act as foothills. Like all older formations, their curves are gentler and their slopes less steep. Their landscape is chequered with ancient towns and villages on hill-tops; they point south to their limit at Tivoli and the Campagna; their valleys nourish the sheep in winter and the grape in summer. Such a land, it seemed, might well satisfy my two demands; of leisurely travel in pre-Roman Italy; and the prospect, at the end, of the square of St. Peter's, crowded with pilgrims, in the great year of the Catholic calendar, Holy Year, 1950.

On my arrival therefore in May at Terni, on the northern borders of the Sabines, I accosted all peasants entering the town with donkeys and asked if I might hire one of their animals for three months to go to Rome. It sounded perhaps rather an odd question. And their replies were not encouraging. How could I feed it? They needed theirs for collecting wood just now, in the summer. Why couldn't I go to Rome anyway by bus? There was an excellent service.

Not even the considerable sums I offered, continually raising my price, appeared to have any effect. And when I complained of their lack of initiative to my landlord at the inn, he showed surprise, scorn even, that anyone should *want* to journey in the Sabines, let alone on a donkey. "One can imagine these people going to England," he said. "But why do you come here? Did we not lose the war? Did you not win it?"

He was a Roman.

And when I tried, haltingly, to give my reasons, he criticised my Italian which, he said, was clearly not good enough to serve me in these "savage parts". It was useless to explain that I had come specially to see these savage parts, "to ascend the barren mountains and cross the depopulated plains", as the guide-book says—"to find the bandits and priests and black-eyed virgins of my imagination", I might have added for such persons, he would have assured me, existed only in my imagination. At last, however, he consented to give me the name of a muleteer with a donkey, who occasionally brought him wood, and who might, he thought, be able to oblige, as he had once been co-opted into the British Army. "He speaks English too," he added.

This explains why I found myself the next morning before a black hut on the outskirts of the town, around which bounded a number of small children clad in grey, shrunken vests. I knocked at the door which, after some moments, was opened by a man in a hat, who proved to be the muleteer in question. His face, although a good deal of Italy was written on it, did not immediately prepossess me in his favour, I must confess. He had a beard of about a month's length; a pitted, almost calcined complexion; and a swollen nose which was turned somewhat to one side. His left hand seemed to be missing and had been replaced by a piece of tattered leather, too shapeless for a glove. In age, he might, like so many Italians of his kind, have been anywhere between forty and seventy. He spoke a difficult dialect; and I began to understand the doubts of my innkeeper.

He did not ask me in but, on hearing what I wanted, took me behind the shack, where he pointed to a donkey which was tethered, standing motionless and silent. He struck this animal several times with a stick, rather as a conjuror might, saying loudly, "*Un bravo somaro! un bravo somaro!"* without however causing it to flinch, or even to blink. He then asked how much I was prepared to pay.

I named a deliberately low figure, which he waved aside, making another suggestion. We then began bargaining, surrounded by a growing audience of peasants, loafers and other quidnuncs. To my question whether it was feasible for a foreigner who spoke little Italian to travel like this in the Sabines, he replied with a term which, I have since found, is often used by Italians when they see doubt or mistrust exhibited, *"Non dubbiti, Signore!"*

He appeared most anxious to accompany me, and although his English seemed to go no further than the words "knife", "spoon" and "saddle", it was clear that the prospect of making some money would keep him helpful and obliging.

It was therefore agreed that he, Giuseppe Masceri, his donkey Pepe, and I, should set out two days later for Rome; and that I should pay half the stipulated sum before leaving—the rest to be delivered at the end of the journey.

The mountainous land in which we proposed to travel has, from early times been a country of shepherds. The Sabine Hills have never offered much agriculturally to the inhabitants, possessing most of the disadvantages of the Alps and few of their benefits—owing to the continental climate and inferior soil. This is probably the chief reason why the eastern portion of Lazio and almost all the Abruzzi behind it, has always been one of the most backward parts of Italy—a land where the advantages of civilisation have long been wanting and where Nature has spread, with some profusion, both her beauty and her curses. Thriving cities once existed here, but like the affair of the Sabine women, they belong to an almost legendary epoch, and few traces of them remain. In the most forested part the bear and the wolf still rove. But this does not prevent the flocks from going up in summer to the higher ground, in search of shade and pasture.

We left at seven o'clock one sunny morning and began the ascent towards Piediluco and the northern Sabines. Masceri indicated that I should mount the donkey. But on my replying that I preferred to walk, being in need of exercise, he was appalled. He, a *cafone*, mounted, he said! And I, a *signore*, on foot! It took me several days to persuade him that our journey must be conducted in this democratic manner, sharing alike. But even then, he never entirely accustomed himself to it. He was happiest loping alongside, holding the rope; while I sat perched above, surveying the bare and stony landscape of the Apennines.

He appeared surprised too that I should wish to strike east first, into the mountainous region of the Abruzzi. He knew that region well enough himself, he said, but in terms of work, not pleasure. It was here, in his youth, that he had earned his living as woodcutter and carrier. "When I was young," he said, trying to discourage me, "there were robbers and wolves in the Abruzzi."

"Excellent!" I said.

"But not now. They were all cleared up in the Fascist reforms."

"I expect," I said, "that they will come back now that Italy has a democratic government like ours again."

"Are there wolves in England, then?" he asked.

I tried to give him some account of our English countryside.

Our first day's journey took us up into the hills behind the *Cascate di Marmora*, bound for the villages of the northern Sabines, with our first goal, Rieti—the ancient Reate of the Romans—three days distant.

Far away on one side gleamed the lake of Piediluco and on the other, almost as blue this cloudless morning, the crests of the Apennines ranging inland. Soon we were away from the roads, moving south under a scorching sun, in a bare land of little hills and mamelons covered with thyme, rosemary, and asphodel. A few olive-trees, one or two almonds, twisted, blackened, shooting out of the stony waste; in the cracks of the rocks, some wild fig-trees; these completed a calcined landscape inhabited exclusively, it appeared, by goats, cigales and donkeys.

Our donkey, Pepe, was a sturdy beast of about eight hands, imperturbable and of a pleasant enough disposition when not going downhill. I was soon to learn than you may present such a donkey with almost any upward slope, however steep; load it with yourself, both of you (as we sometimes did), and it will not make a sound of protest. Nothing short of its legs actually collapsing under the load will stop its grunting progress upwards and forwards. Present this beast with a downward slope however; dismount; ease its burden; lead it; coax it; cajole it; and it will utter sounds of protest, brayings and whinnyings, as if about to expire. On these occasions, Masceri lengthened the leading rope, moving some yards ahead, while I went well to the side, out of range of its hind legs, which if they missed their footing, were liable to kick. This technique I was to master.

We approached the famous waterfalls of Marmora our first morning. They must have changed greatly since Childe Harold ecstasised over them. First, they have been turned into a source of electrical power for all Lazio. And, secondly, in 1944, this electrical plant was "carpet-bombed". Fragments of twisted girder now poke out of heaps of masonry and concrete, lie on the ground or hang drunkenly from roofless buildings, between dynamos and generators, extinct and rusty. Acres of buildings lie open to the elements. Hens, pigs and chickens totter about it all, under the vague supervision of the only member of the staff who remains—the watchman whose job, like that of so many other custodians in Italy, is to look after ruins. We spoke to this man. But he showed little interest either in the past, present or future of his charge, intent only on collecting wood from a nearby thicket. Nor were the falls themselves in action.

"The water," he explained briefly, "is being retained until June, when the generator in Terni starts again."

I was unable to understand how a waterfall can be "retained". Whereupon he pointed to a large vertical pipe running down from the top, which flanked the dried-up falls.

Down this piece of metal then rushed the water that once caused Byron to add four cantos to his epical poem!

After these falls, which are situated in the valley of the Nera, we walked upward through groves of deciduous trees, interspersed here and there with a myrtle or ilex to remind us that we were still in southern climes. Nothing could be more picturesque than this valley. Steep hills, in part almost precipitous, surrounded us. With that extraordinary contrast of climate and vegetation to be found only in Italy, we crossed at intervals purling brooks, full of the melting snow of the mountains—and yet only a few hours later we were to find ourselves again in the torrid landscape of southern Provence.

Here and there, high on a rock or promontory, stood the solitary remains of some castle, a relic of the time when a feudal baron dwelt there with his ruffianly soldiers and received his lord, the Emperor, on his way to Rome—places which once commanded the countryside, often terrorised it. Now they are blackened hulks with wild plants growing in the walls,

the home of strident bats and ravens. Towards dusk
we stopped at the foot of one in the high ground
near Labro, and I climbed up to get a view of the
countryside. I walked about the walls to the accompaniment of the crickets who now inhabit them. Here
a baronial family once sat entrenched, with all its
privileges, rights and barbarous passions, meting out
summary justice to vassals and serfs—creatures to
whom it assured food and shelter and who, in return,
obeyed its smallest whim. From here a baron levied
war on his neighbours with the sovereignty of a king.

It was hot and sultry and, on reaching the topmost
walls, I sat down and looked out towards the great
plain of Rieti in its bowl of mountains ahead. Nowhere
could a better impression of the land we were to travel
in be obtained. Two great *cordigliere* or chains of
parallel mountains ran away south, joining twenty
miles away, to form a bowl containing a fertile area,
with the town of Rieti at the end. To the sides of this
bowl clung little villages or other ruined castles, walled,
sometimes moated, all testifying by their position on
spur or mamelon to that word "defence", used as
much then as it is to-day (and which was also, then
as now, often only another word for "attack").

The inhabitants of these villages have, in the course
of centuries, cultivated not only the fertile area in the
basin, but its sides as well; and the agriculture seems
to run right up until the bare rock allows no more.
The houses in the villages, huddled together one on
top of the other, repeat the design in vertical terms.
It was in one of these villages, Labro, which I now saw
some miles to the left, that we proposed to spend the
night.

Before descending I saw that phenomenon, known
well enough in the Alps—the illumination of the highest
crests with a purple glow a quarter of an hour before
dawn, and the prolongation of that light a quarter of

B

an hour after dusk. The whole line of the Apennines, with the rising mount of Terminillo in front, lit up in this strange glow, stretching clearly south in the evening air, until it was lost in the horizon fifty miles away. And then, as if at some hidden signal, the campanile of the villages in the valley began to sound the *Ave Maria.*

To reach the village of Labro in the failing light we followed a tortuous path in the rock, among lentisque plants and myrtles, meeting occasionally shepherds or donkeys returning for the night. The flocks moved along in a cloud of dust, directed by shaggy dogs, their shepherds sometimes mounted like ourselves, more often on foot. I walked along beside one of these flocks for a while, and had for a moment the impression of living in some idyllic past.

Our arrival in Labro however, quickly dispelled this romantic illusion. An agglomeration of dwellings of a most primitive kind, some with dunghills at their doors, announced the entry to the village. Immense swine stalked about, intermingled with half-naked children. The interior of the cabins revealed, through open doors, glimpses of low, vaulted rooms, like caves; the stab of dark eyes pierced us as we passed. Labro was silent, except for the sound of the returning mule hooves, ringing out sharp on the rock and *pavé* in the dusk. It seemed depopulated. And I wondered if it was becoming one of those Italian villages which, in the course of centuries, slowly lose their population, until their walls, like those of the castle I had just visited, become simply a habitation for goats and lizards, and other more fundamental, indestructible species; a village which dies a natural death—instead of the usual violent destruction in Italy, by earthquake, pestilence or at the hands of man.

That it was still alive however, if in a rather inert way, was proved by the species of *trattoria* we slept in, which stood almost at the top of the village. It was a two-storied building, square and ugly, redeemed only by a little garden with a hedge of prickly-pears in front; and an olive-wood table at which I ate that evening a meal of *polenta* and spaghetti, and drank a thick dark wine. Any misgivings I had about coming to Labro were soon dispelled by the wonderful view from my bedroom across the valley of Rieti that night; and by the freshness of the air and the scents of acacia which came in through the window while I slept.

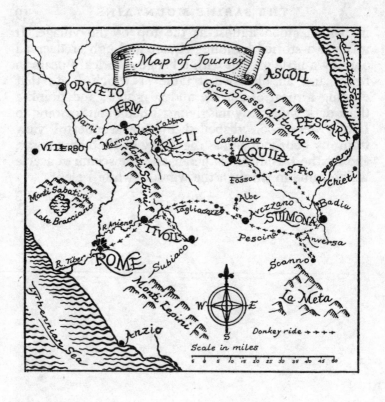

CHAPTER TWO

Rieti

I WOKE THE NEXT morning to find Masceri already at the door saddling the donkey, in brilliant sunshine. The blueness of the sky augured well for our journey down to Rieti, and by seven o'clock we were on the road. It lay among the high ground to the north of the valley, among olive-groves interspersed with hedges of eucalyptus and shrubs in flower. The olive-trees of central Italy are not as big as the giant brand of southern France and the Riviera—where perhaps the marine air has some influence on their size. Small, sober and tenacious, they renounce all attempts at foliage, confining themselves strictly to producing fruit. Visiting Frenchmen blaspheme at the Italian olive, calling it a second-rate willow or an imitation shrub. But its oil is as good as anything on the *Côte d'Azur*.

A *scirocco* had replaced the mildness of the previous day, and at a solitary farmhouse on a southward-facing brow, we were glad to stop at midday to eat and drink—some of the salami and cheese and black bread I had brought with me, while the owner offered us a glass of his white wine. It was pleasant to drink this wine drawn, he told us, from the vines that climbed about the trellis-work above the table.

He was most communicative—in some ways, a remarkable man. He did not grouse about the old times and say they were better! A contented Italian peasant! I tried to find out why; and he told me that some months before he had been granted the ownership of his land. "And if you're going into Rieti," he said, "you'll find the place in an uproar. I was one of the lucky ones last time. But the peasants have marched again. The landlords will have to sell again."

I had heard before that these land riots were going on all over southern Italy. Most of them, people said, were justified, for the peasants suffered from absentee landlords and exorbitant rents. What discouraged them most was that the land was owned by rich proprietors in Rome and controlled by their bailiffs. These men fixed the price of all commodities; the number of days the peasants might work, sometimes as few as ninety in a year; and generally let the area get into a state of decay which the industrious Italian peasant, given a chance, would soon rectify.

It always seems to me surprising that this should suit the book of the proprietors—to limit their production. I asked the man about it; but he could not explain why. "If they do not give way," was all he would say darkly, "there will be a revolution. Like the French one."

But no doubt, I thought, those absentee landlords in Rome know the amiable temper of their countrymen—better at any rate than the French aristocrats knew theirs in 1789. For riots in Italy seldom last longer than an hour and the rioters are, after all, Italians—good-natured people whose habits as warriors are so mild and as civilians so wild, that the difference between war and peace, order and civil strife, is not really very great.

I was not surprised that this peasant no longer grumbled about his own condition. He had all that a Greek philosopher could have desired—a comfortable if modest hearth, under an everlasting sun, fanned by the breezes of the south; a small vineyard; a goat, a couple of kids; some sheep and fowls. Such a man is not likely to remain a revolutionary for long.

We now set out on one of the finest walks I have ever made. Behind rose the majestic amphitheatre of the Apennines, burnt and wild, and to the west the

Sabine foothills—a view stretching away this lucid afternoon right into Lazio—a typically Mediterranean landscape of ilexes and evergreen oaks, where the mad cigales sing all day on the powdery olives.

Climbing these slopes just before midday, we came upon a forest in the middle of this arid landscape; and not of meagre pines and ilexes, but thick with oaks and chestnuts as if, by some prodigy, the woodland of England had suddenly appeared beneath the sun and sky of Italy.

This phenomenon is not unusual in a Mediterranean landscape, however, where an underground river still flows beneath a parched and calcined mountain. Most of the rivers dry up in summer, but the subterranean ones form a sort of reservoir, capable of nourishing all manner of deciduous life above. We entered and were immediately absorbed into an atmosphere of freshness and silence; the very air changed into something cool and odorous. It was as if we had entered one of those sacred groves, which the axe of the ancients was never permitted to profane. *Est nemus Aemoniae!*

Stretched out beneath these oaks, we enjoyed one of the finest panoramas in the world. Not a tree, not a housetop broke the wide monotony of the mountains. The grass running away from the wood was soon yellow, the weeds parched; and where there had been wayside pools in winter the ground was cracked and dry. For nearly an hour we lay like this, until the afternoon heat had lessened, and we could begin our descent into the valley of Rieti. The lower slopes, which had been invisible from the wood, now revealed signs of human activity—huts with thatched roofs, a solitary monastery hidden behind a curtain of oaks and elms, some farmhouses in grey stone, and a mill placed above a stream. Where there is water in central Italy in summer-time there is always life; and a quantity of cattle, sheep and goats moved in the nearby meadows.

This valley of Rieti used once to be a lake, the centre of the Sabine country. But in 290 B.C. the Sabines were conquered by Rome and the consul, Manius Dentatus, with characteristic efficiency, immediately drained it. Since then it has always been famous as an oasis of pasture among the burnt and dusty ranges of the Apennines. Cicero, who used to come up to Rieti for law-suits, likens it to the verdant vale of Tempe in Thessaly. And eleven hundred years later St. Francis selected it, as the spot from which to propagate his faith.

Of its ancient capital, the Reate of the Sabines, nothing remains. The modern city, Rieti, is still partly surrounded by walls, perhaps on the site of the pre-Roman ones, but they are of a much later period. It is pleasantly situated on the right bank of the Velino at the southern end of the valley. Its history, since those early times, has always been of a most turbulent kind. Sacked by the Lombards, burnt by the Saracens, sacked again by Ruggero II of Normandy —its story is that of most southern Italian towns.

We arrived here on our third day. And I soon remembered the words of the contented peasant who had spoken of the land riots. We had not been in Rieti more than thirty-six hours when some excitement started in the piazza. Men began running about, shopkeepers let down their metal *saraceni* blinds, and white-faced women stood at doorways. The *nucleo celere* or flying squad appeared, and began directing affairs from a jeep in the centre of the square, by loudspeaker. They all had sub-machine guns in their hands. I asked the hotel-keeper what was happening.

"There has been a meeting of the peasants," he said. "They were about to march on the *municipio* and demand more land. But the police have collared the ringleaders. Look!" He pointed to a police-truck which had just drawn up, in which two bedraggled peasants sat under guard. "The trouble is," he said, "that they

never catch the real Communists. They only catch
poor fellows like those, who have really done no harm."

"What will happen to them?"

"A night or two in gaol. Until it is proved that they
are quite harmless."

On my asking how long this would go on for, he
showed considerable scorn for the riot, and said it
would all be over by midnight. "It's caused by the
Festa dell' Unità, a sort of Communist jamboree they're
holding this week," he said. "They'll forget it this
evening when they go into the public gardens. There'll
be popular dances, women and fireworks."

That evening after dinner, I decided to see this
Festa dell' Unità for myself; I had heard it was a
regular feature of all Italian towns to-day.

I joined a happy throng of people in the main street
with flags and red hats, all moving towards the public
gardens, where a large poster announced that a *Festa
per la Pace* would take place this night. Although
I did my best at the entry gate in Italian, it was clear
to the officials that I was a foreigner. On these occasions,
I usually pass myself off as a journalist.

"You have a journalist's pass?" said a young man
with horn-rimmed spectacles, just like a French
intellectual.

I said I had not. Some colleagues appeared and a
discussion took place about me.

"You are for the Party of Progress?" said one of
them, after some time.

I had to confess I was not. "But permit me to add,"
I said, "that neither am I for the Party of Reaction."

"What are you, then?"

"A traveller. Interested in the Italian people."

The word "people" seemed to satisfy them. And I
was allowed to enter beneath the triumphal arch and
mingle with the wine-drinking, sausage-sucking, grape-
spitting crowd, which seemed to me for all the world

like any other Italian crowd—good-natured, boisterous and inclined to be musical.

It was indeed the music that first struck me in this Communist gathering. At each brightly-lighted little stall, where all manner of foodstuffs, lottery tickets, trials of strength and Aunt Sally shies, were being peddled with the commercial briskness for which the Italians are famous, a loud-speaker gave out airs from *Manon Lescaut*, interspersed with American jazz. I was surprised at one place to come upon a species of Hyde Park orator on a soap-box, who appeared to be making some political point. He was surrounded by a merry mob, who could not have heard one word he was saying.

I stopped at a book-stall which contained revolutionary matter, and thumbed some of the pages. Whereupon a brisk little old woman in a dirty pinafore appeared from behind and hissed feverishly: "Study! Study! Study!!! Young man, you will soon have need of all your knowledge."

At nearby tables sat the *giovanotti*, the smart youths of the boulevard, in their spruce pullovers and bunched-up ties, reeking that subtle breath of brilliantine, sweat and petrol, to be found wherever a number of young Italians and their bikes come together. Being still hungry, I sat at a table and ordered a *pizza*—that Neapolitan dish beloved by Neapolitans, artists and tourists, and in whose favour little can be said, save that it is cheap. A torchlight procession was being organised in an adjacent field, and shortly after, to the sound of trumpet, trombone and drum, it set out, bound for I knew not where. Most of the youths at the tables adjusted their hats and joined it. They were merry in that Italian way, without being drunk. They left one youth in charge of their motor-bikes, which were secured with a number of padlocks and chains. The procession passed right before my table where I now sat alone, smoking a cigarette and sipping

my wine—by a coincidence facing them as they
marched past, so that I felt like some blasé general
reviewing his troops. Something in this manner perhaps
annoyed the youth guarding the bikes, standing at
attention as they went by. Perhaps I should have
stood up; for afterwards he came over to me. "Your
nationality, *signore?*" he said, in a not very friendly
voice.

"English."

"May I ask your business here?"

"You may. I am a journalist."

"A writer?" He became less hostile. And I remembered that a writer is often a synonym in the Latin
countries for an intellectual; and an intellectual even
more often a synonym for a Communist. It seemed
to please him, and when we had talked for some time
about Communists, he seemed to think I was one. He
told me of certain changes he would like to see introduced into the Constitution of Italy. He then called
over some friends and told them about me, and as
we talked they were all soon smiling, convinced that
I was against God, King and Country. They invited
me to a drink and became most friendly. Even when,
on the Sicilian asking me what alterations I would like
to see effected in my own country, I reminded him
that in his own country of old, at Syracuse, he who
wished to propose modifications to the laws used to
have to present himself before the magistrature with a
rope around his neck—even when I pointed this out,
they only roared with laughter. They displayed all
the charm and hospitality for which their race is
famous, escorting me later to a confectioner's stall,
where they treated me to an ice-cream and a small cup
of very black coffee. And then suddenly one of them
pointed to a tall, well-built man standing in conversation outside a tent. "The Onorevole Piccini!" he cried;
and he went over to him, beckoning me to follow.

"He is an old friend," he said. "I will present you."

This man was, I knew from the newspapers, quite a well-known politician—a most persistent critic of the Government at Monte Citorio, the Roman parliament. But although a politician, he looked just like a German professor. Spectacles, it is said, are seldom wanting in the portrait of a German professor; and this man had the thickest lenses I have ever seen in my life, like blocks of quartz. What he can have seen out of them, I could not imagine. When I was introduced he said—before I had even opened my mouth—yes, he would be delighted to answer any questions, if I would kindly step inside the tent.

With my friend I did so, and we found ourselves in a small tent with photographs of famous revolutionary figures of world importance on the walls. In appearance, this Italian politician was not unprepossessing. The face was large and massive, but on the whole dignified; the eyebrows knit, the nose aquiline. "Now what," he said, turning to me, "do you wish to ask?"

I tried desperately to think of something, arriving finally at nothing better than this rather lame question: "Do you think there will be a war?"

He had clearly dealt with this before. He settled down and after a preliminary cough, explained the world situation. His long and continuous contact with audiences caused him to address himself, perhaps unconsciously, to an imaginary public; and whenever he put a rhetorical question, which was fairly often, I felt it would be better not to reply. He quoted easily from memory—names, places, dates. Sometimes he traced in the air with his fingers certain signs, as if to place them on an invisible world map; a town, a region, a country. . . .

Through the half-open windows of the tent came in the warm evening air, rustling and swelling the curtains. A part was in darkness, and it was to this area, rather than to me, that he addressed himself, as if here was the real, invisible audience. He started with the world situation. He said that he, personally, did not believe in the inevitability of a conflict, but that, at the moment, "the chances of a world conflagration were somewhat greater than those of indefinite peace." This was due to the fact that the world was changing, social conditions were improving, etc. ". . . and although in the circumstances," he finished, "complete accord seems unlikely for some time among the Big Five at Flushing and Success, the recent exchange of ideas and reciprocal suggestions leads me to hope that important decisions, of perhaps epoch-making importance for the future of humanity, may shortly be realised."

What surprised me particularly was the moderation of his language. I had always heard that Italian politicians are exceptionally violent, vituperative men, calling their opponents "vermin", "reactionary scum", and so on. But this man had the finished, ambiguous language of a British diplomat. I thanked him, and assuring him that my own countrymen were equally interested in the preservation of world peace, I took my leave.

My new friends met us outside and I was presented with a large red cockade. We then watched a display of fireworks, some of which wrote ingenious slogans in the sky; after which I danced with a pretty peasant girl in a snood. And then at a table, we all drank a series of toasts together (could one, after their hospitality, refuse?)—to Italy; to England; to the Liberation that would come; and to the Peace that would follow. After that, they accompanied me back to my hotel, singing, only stopping once on the way to point out a small shrine which has recently been transformed into a cemetery in which, they said, rest the bones of eleven Partisans, who blew up a German armoured train in 1944. To whose souls be peace.

CHAPTER THREE

A Rock Town

"EXCURSIONS", SAYS *BAEDEKER*, "may be made from Rieti to the picturesque mountain scenery of the Central Apennines, though not unattended by difficulties, on account of the indifferent character of the inns and roads."

We now had opportunity to confirm this pleasant little euphemism, and I began to understand Masceri's reluctance to leave the straight and narrow ways of Umbria. A morning's journey brought us along muddy tracks to the village of Poggio Bustone, where St. Francis used to live as a hermit. It is isolated on the side of a mountain, at a considerable height, clinging almost precariously to the rock. It consists of about five ancient and dirty alleys, ladder-streets which one has to scale rather than walk up, with shrines at street-corners and large, yellowish jars under the house eaves, used apparently as cisterns. A stay of a week here would give one, I should think, some of the agility of the goats which are as much a feature of its streets as of the mountainside. When we arrived, the little piazza was swarming with morose men, lounging and gossiping—among whom shawled women strode about efficiently, sometimes with jars on their heads. Goats fed ubiquitously on garbage in the side streets, some rampant on tubs of water-melon peelings. Poultry pecked and scraped. And before one house stood the milkman with his mobile milkcan, a nanny-goat being tranquilly tapped. Bits of lemon peel strung together on strings hung drying from the eaves, with festoons of macaroni dangling beside them.

"Why, *signorino*, did you come here?" said Masceri
pathetically.

I had come for a very good reason. This place,
together with Greccio on the other side of the valley,
is one of the great Franciscan shrines of Italy. Most
people imagine that Assisi was the chief, indeed the
only, seat of the Saint. But it was from here, in the
valley of Rieti, the *sacred valley* as it is now called,
that the *poverello* addressed his loudest plea to the
world. He inhabited four different hermitages on these
valley sides, of which the most famous and inaccessible
is this one, above Poggio Bustone.

Another five hundred feet above the village, a climb
up an almost vertical mountainside brought me that
afternoon to the small, granite shrine in the rocks
where he used to live. Here he would spend days
alone in meditation and prayer, lying on the rocks of
the Apennines, coloured like them in his brown
peasant's serge, while mice and lizards ran over him
and nibbled bread-crumbs from his wallet. Here
Brother Grasshopper and Sister Cricket spoke to him.
And here—so the monks in the convent below told
me—he used to escape when his fame was established
and too many admirers and sycophants came to see
him in the village. In the convent of these monks are
a number of paintings of St. Francis up here on the
rocks, one of which represents him as a *bienheureux*,
rolling himself in a bed of nettles, in order to forget
the vision of a beautiful woman, who is also depicted
most graphically to the left of the picture.

The most famous moment in the history of
Poggio Bustone, was that morning in 1208, the 4th
October, when the Saint descended early from his
hermitage and was seen by the villagers, to whom he
had never spoken before, going about the one main
street, uttering a remark which is now commemorated
with a plaque. While of no particular originality it is

extremely amiable: "*Buon giorno, buona gente!*" It was shortly after this that he also accomplished the miracle of the Poggio Bustone vines. A mob of excited admirers broke through the cordon to see him, and trampled all over the only village vineyard, completely destroying it. But that autumn the vines produced exactly the same yield of excellent grapes as they had in the previous ones.

It was now nearly midday, and we decided to look for an eating-place. But the few shops that were open stocked apparently nothing but *caccio*, that goat's cheese, eaten all over central and southern Italy, which makes the eater smell for hours after like a billy-goat himself.

"Let us at least find a *trattoria*," I said, for I was ravenously hungry. But on asking quite politely, we were met with such sullen looks and scowls that I felt we must have offended these people in some way—as if to eat their food was to deprive them of it. Loutish and heavy, with features vacant and devoid of expression, they stared at us. Was I, I asked myself, still in Italy? Their thick, coarse pronunciation sounded like some Scotch or German peasant attempting to express himself in the language of the Peninsula. I wondered if I had stumbled on one of those little communities descended throughout the ages from the Lombards, untouched by the land save for her tongue. Whatever it was, they certainly lacked the hospitality for which the Italians are famous. Indeed, the fierce and bigoted spirit of the late Dictator still seemed to pervade this little place.

At last—for I was so hungry I could have eaten stones—I went up to a young man who had seemed for a moment to smile at us, and offered him a hundred *lire* if he would lead us to an eating place. He consented and led us down a series of side-streets to a woman who, he said, "cooks for visitors". On reaching a corner, he pointed vaguely to a staircase inside a house and then, having received his fee, hastened from us. I followed his directions, not without a suspicion however, that he might be deceiving me.

At the top of the stairs inside, we ran into a bulky man who was descending. He said he was the husband of the woman who cooked, and would obtain some wine for us while his wife prepared the meal. This was clearly one of those Italian hostelries that hang out no sign, that never expect and never reject a guest. Such a reception however, revived our spirits; and although the *padrona* was a very meagre-looking person (her size in Italy generally indicates the quality of the food), we gladly took our places in their bed-sitting-dining-room. The husband was a fiery, red-faced man who spoke, he said, excellent English. This was not so. But he was extremely friendly, claiming to know the English well, for he had spent three years among them as a captive in Kenya. He bore us no resentment for this; on the contrary, he spoke of it almost with relish, and seemed anxious only to return to it. He was most interested to learn that I too had been a soldier. I told him we had had some difficulty among his townsfolk in finding his house.

"What boorishness!" he said. "These people are coarse, ignorant, uneducated peasants. May I apologise on their behalf to two persons come from afar." And, placing his hand over his heart, he got up and made a low bow. "They have just been rioting and claiming a redistribution of lands. The only excuse I fear, I can offer for such conduct to a man from the country of the great Henderson."

"Henderson?" I said.

"Exactly. The first progressivist Foreign Minister of our times." He then explained that he had read much during his confinement in Kenya, in particular works dealing with British Socialism—and had been

c

greatly struck by the speeches of Arthur Henderson. "Had that man had his way," he said, "there would have been no war in 1939. But alas, the poor fellow was dead when they started it! The Fascist scoundrels!"

"You are then, I take it," I said, "a Communist!"

He was much wounded at this suggestion. "By no means!" he said. "I hate them. I am, if I may so flatter myself, a British Socialist. That is why I so admire England. The country that has always been ahead in social reform. You have read the works of Henderson?"

I said I had not. (I did not even know that he had written any.)

"No? Strange! A great man, a *very* great man! He will, I claim, still be read a hundred years hence. I consider that in his political thought we find combined the genius of Plato, Marcus Aurelius and Dante."

"The first two," I said, "I do not doubt. But Dante? You surprise me. Surely, was Henderson a poet?"

"I can see," he said, getting up, "that you are unfamiliar with his finest works. I shall get them for you."

But fortunately at this point his wife arrived with the food, and he began to help her lay the table.

The meal consisted of a large bowl of broth made from the famous *caccio*, followed by a meat dish, also of goat-stew. Now, any part of this animal is extremely distasteful to me, and I asked Masceri in an undertone if he thought we would get anything else. For answer, he nodded his head, crossed himself, and fell on it like a shark.

"*Non dubbiti, signore!*" he replied.

I decided to be courageous and ask for something else. The woman said this would be possible and returned a few minutes later with a small, roasted pigeon which had clearly died of starvation, surrounded by some of the most evil-looking carrots and onions I have ever seen in my life. Even the Count Ugolino would have turned up his nose at this. I therefore returned to the goat-stew, which I ate under the benevolent eye of the red-faced man. He informed me with pride that, in the matter of food, his village was self-sufficient; the amount of imported food was negligible. (To the fastidious traveller, I thought, sadly so.) He then drew up a chair and said, "I will now tell you of my war experiences, which you, as a British military man, will undoubtedly find of exceptional interest."

Then in a long, rambling account, half in English, half in Italian, he told us of the events which had led up to his capture in Abyssinia in 1941, after he had been decorated three times for exceptional bravery. He had no sooner finished this, and I was thinking of going before he began again, when Masceri, who had drunk nearly an entire flask of wine, said, "Would it interest you non-commissioned officers to hear how a poor, simple Italian private was captured in Sicily?"

The red-faced man appeared little attracted by this —nor indeed was I. But Masceri had begun. . . .

"I was near Trapani," he said, dramatically, "on the beach. It was dusk! The officer had told us that the position was of no importance, and that a battle would be unnecessary because we were about to be surrounded. Suddenly, we saw coming out of the water in the bay—a submarine! It was like a sea monster! At first we thought it was Italian. But then it began shooting. The officer said we were to retire behind the house and await orders. . . ."

"Were you supposed to be defending Trapani?" said the red-faced man sarcastically.

"Yes. And no. The officer had said that the Germans had taken the best positions behind. And as I have said, there would *not be a battle*. But after waiting half an hour, when nothing happened, we went out again. To have a look. And what do you think we saw?

That submarine had turned into a tank! Into two tanks! Three! All coming up out of the water towards us."

"Our amphibious vessels," I said proudly.

"Yes. And they could go on the beach! And shooting all the time!"

"What did you do then?" said the red-faced man, suddenly becoming interested in these technical details.

"What could we do?" said Masceri pathetically. "The Germans had taken all our ammunition. There was only one thing, the officer said. Surrender. For after the tanks came the Tommies." He turned to me. "They gave us all battle-dresses and liberated us. And that is how I worked for the R.A.S.C. Do you," he said to the red-faced man, "know what R.A.S.C. means?"

"No," said our host.

"It means, Royal—Army—Service—Corps," said Masceri in almost incomprehensible English.

"All the same," said the red-faced man, "your behaviour seems to me to have been pretty bad. You hadn't any rifles, you say. Then where were your other weapons? Those Sicilians should have been able to slit a few throats. Where were your bayonets? And your knives?"

"We had had them confiscated," said Masceri complacently.

The red-faced man looked at me again. "Huh!" he said scornfully.

Shortly after this, I managed to tear myself away. Our host would have gone on talking about the war indefinitely, and was most sorry to see us go. He said he would tell his wife to feed us as long as we liked; and if we should return at any time, or if any of my friends should be in these parts, he hoped we would eat again in his house. This I promised to do, at the same time determining to guard against such a possibility.

CHAPTER FOUR

On Being German

OUR WAY AFTER Rieti led always upward, through regions of changing vegetation; first, vines and olives; then shrub and deciduous trees; and finally, pines—a strange contrast, the almost Sicilian countryside of the valley and then, four hours later, the wooded slopes of Scotland. For these mountains are deceptive, in the manner of all primary formations. Gentle, undulating and innocuous in appearance, they present slopes as tiring as anything in the Alps. They seem never to end. One walks on and on, hoping to come out suddenly on a ridge, with the prospect of a welcoming village below. Yet ridge after ridge reveals only further climbs and further mountains, hitherto obscured, all slightly higher. A thousand metres' rise is made without any visible gain to look back upon. And it was not until we had scrambled up and down at least twenty such hillsides, through bramble and gorse, over loose slates and granite blocks, that we came upon the little village of Pizzoli, a cluster of yellowed house-fronts and orange slates in a concealed valley.

Hoping for bread and cheese and drink, we walked into it at 3.30 in the afternoon, and were served some wine which the proprietor assured me was his best, but which tasted like vinegar. He was a small, hirsute man who eyed my knapsack with disapproval. "Germans!" I heard him mutter to a bystander.

I explained that I was English, but he only grudgingly brought the wine, adding that there was nothing to eat. At this I extracted my passport, which I flourished, hoping that its escutcheon might at least produce some cheese. He examined it without enthusiasm, and on his turning it upside down, I realised that he could not read. Meanwhile a crowd of beggars, urchins and knitting grannies had come in and were examining me with interest and disapproval. I began to feel uncomfortable, conscious of that dislike of the meddling stranger which is supposed to characterise all mountain peoples.

"The Germans shot five of our young men before they left in 1944," grumbled the innkeeper to his friend at the counter. "Put them up against the wall there. Outside." He pointed to the window. "You could see it all from here."

So *that* was it! I had found before in Italy that I must have something Teutonic in my appearance. It is axiomatic that an Englishman never travels here in anything meaner than a very large motor-car. And a person like myself, on foot or donkey, is simply taken for a German student.

And so, after the further appearance of a villainous and threatening-looking member of the local *carabinieri*, and in spite of our hunger, Masceri and I decided to leave. I put the pack on the donkey, and followed by forty pairs of staring eyes, we moved on, unsustained and unnourished by the little village of Pizzoli. Even the geese were rude to us as we left and hissed; but not, I think, because I was German. Italian geese, I have always found, are bad-mannered everywhere, impertinent creatures who wander about unreproved and snap at passers-by. They seem never to have forgotten the Capitoline incident. (Nor indeed have the Italians, to whom they might be as sacred as a Hindoo cow.)

Little villages like this, buried in the mountains, are notable for the unpredictable welcome they may give you. Living within themselves, untouched by outside affairs, they form their own opinions, very naturally, from their own experience. Where the Germans had behaved better, we should no doubt have been well received.

It is worth while at all events, to make up one's mind, when travelling on foot in Italy, that one is German.

But shortly after leaving, the reason for this hostility, or at least some of it, became clear. We were following a mounting path along a dusty track, occasionally meeting a shepherd or a goat, when we were suddenly confronted at the top of the hill with a small, green construction painted in streaks of faded green and brown—a pillbox; now more naturally camouflaged by the brambles and ivy that had climbed up around it in the last five years. It had a door of solid iron, as wide as a bank's strong-room, and walls about three yards thick.

A peep inside, where a smell of indescribable filth assaulted me, told that it had now another, more Italian, function—to shelter urchins, goats and beggars. We heard sepulchral grunts and groans, but I withdrew too quickly to tell if they were from man or beast.

Masceri sniffed around it. "Huh, Germans!" he said at length.

I asked how he had learnt to distinguish a German pillbox from that of other nations. (It reminded me of what I had once spent two years building in East Anglia.)

"Look!" he said, pointing to a sign still clearly visible in big black letters near the door: EINTRITT VERBOTEN! ENTRATA VIETATA!

It amazed me to think that anyone should ever *want* to enter such a place, confirmed though it was by the sounds within.

Walking on among the gold-flowered broom beyond, we found a whole warren of channels and tunnels and underground passages, linked to one another and leading to other pillboxes, all overgrown with foliage, still bearing the traces of the paint that once covered them.

This then is the latest mark on the Peninsula of that northerner who every hundred years or so, descends into the hot lands, drawn there partly out of scorn for Latin weakness, partly out of envy of Latin ease. And here he stays, generally a few decades, until more urgent affairs at home recall him.

The influence of this recent military activity became even more marked a little later in the evening; and I realised that here, in the memorable but not altogether happily chosen words of our Prime Minister, the Allies had indeed drawn their "red-hot rake up Italy." We were pushing on hopefully—hungrily too, for not a village was in sight. Dusk had come and I was beginning to think we should spend the evening, perhaps the night, without human company, eating the horrible scraps of *caccio* and dried *polenta* Masceri carried in his dirty handkerchief, when the report of a nearby gun awakening echoes in the hills, announced that we were no longer alone.

We stopped and listened, and a minute or two later, a man came out of a thicket on our right. He was carrying a smoking shotgun; and attached to his belt were a brace of birds and a rabbit. It surprised me that shooting should go on like this in the evening, even by full moon (for night had fallen with the rapidity common in these mountainous regions). Such a man must have the eyes of a lynx. As he fell in with our path and seemed to be going the same way, I decided to speak to him, and perhaps ask if there was a village in the vicinity.

He turned his face to me, and it was by no means pleasing; a long, hooked nose, small pig-eyes and—what I liked least of all—a continual, leering smile. He ignored my question.

"I can shoot anything," he said, "even in the dark. Are you an Englishman?"

"You surprise me," I said, as politely as possible.

"Yes, during the war I was the crack shot of the regiment. A Partisan too. I slept by day and they sent me out at night, wandering in the enemy lines. In this way, I killed three one night. One with a bullet and two with my knife." Here he tapped a long, curved knife in his belt.

"Who," I asked, "were the enemy?" (For it is not easy, when talking of the recent wars with Italians, to know who were friend and foe.)

He turned his eyes slowly on me. "The English," he said.

"I am sorry to hear that," I said, "for I am an Englishman myself. And I do not like to hear of my countrymen being killed like this. In the dark."

"Do not fear!" he said, smiling suddenly, "I thought you were English when I saw your face. But the war is over now. See, I put my gun away!" And he thrust it into a canvas case slung over his shoulder and took out a pipe, evidently quite willing to be friends. I suddenly felt, in these bleak surroundings, like Hiawatha when he met an enemy in some vast inane in Manitoba who offered him the pipe of peace.

"It is true," he continued, "that I was in the Italian Army and fought the English. But I later became a Partisan. In these very woods here!" He pointed dramatically around. "And then I killed quite as many Germans as Englishmen. More in fact, I think. . . ." And he began counting on his fingers.

I saw that it was a matter of complete indifference to this man what he was killing, Germans, Englishmen or rabbits, so long as he had a gun in his hand and a knife in his belt.

As he seemed to know these parts well, I asked him what chance we had of finding accommodation.

"Do not fear!" he said. "I know some old friends in Colle. Partisans. They will put you up."

I was not particularly keen on sleeping with a lot of

Partisans. But I was so tired by now that I would have slept with an Arab for a bed. And we walked along for the next hour, in intermittent conversation, largely connected with our respective military pasts.

In this way we came to Colle, another of those fairyland villages in the moonlight, perched alone on the side of an impregnable rock, enchanting from afar, repugnant at closer quarters. It took nearly half an hour to ascend its steep and grassless slopes, and we found ourselves in a place where a street lamp was unknown and everyone had gone to bed. We lumbered down a side-street, and before a featureless two-storied building our new friend uttered hoarse sounds, calculated to stir his friends. After some moments a woman put a shock of hair out.

"I am an old friend of Mario Collodi, who used to live here," bawled the hunter. "Can you tell me where he lives? These gentlemen want accommodation."

"Mario Collodi! Mario is dead for all I know, or care," said the woman rudely. "A noisy creature like yourself, disturbing respectable people. Go away! Everyone is asleep!"

Having seen the inertness of the village, at this point I intervened—in desperation. "*Signora!*" I pleaded. "*Please* tell us where we can get a room!"

The woman appeared equally unimpressed by me and was about to withdraw, when there was a movement behind and a fat, sleepy man with a candle appeared and pushed her aside. "Who is that speaking?" he said. "Why, that strange accent can only belong to young Adolf, the German prisoner who used to mend the tractor! Have you come back, boy? You have certainly come at the right time. It broke again only yesterday. Wait! I will let you in!". . .

This was not the first, nor was it to be the last, time that I have been taken for an Adolf in Italy; but never

with a more pleasing result. For our host, in spite of
perceiving his error when he came down, had not the
heart to turn us away. He led us to a barn behind
the house, where he brought us hay and straw and,
to my surprise, when I had dossed down, a bowl of
soup! After drinking this I arranged the straw, lay
down and attempted to sleep. But I found it difficult.
Farmyard noises multiplied. A cow was tethered
behind the barn, snuffling. A pig passed, grunting
thoughtfully. Somewhere not far away an animal,
perhaps a horse, munched hay. Then I fell asleep. . . .
I can therefore vouch that the *Jupiter Hospitalis* of the
Romans, under whose auspice no traveller could be
turned away at night, is not dead in the Sabine Hills.

CHAPTER FIVE

An Earthquake-Lover

AQUILA, THE CAPITAL of the province, which we approached on the twelfth day of our journey, is situated in the shadow of the Gran Sasso. It is one of the highest cities in Italy. During the Middle Ages it was no more than a castle clinging defiantly to the side of the great mountain, although even then one of the most important fortresses on the road north. It was built in 1140 by Frederick II of Hohenstaufen, to reunite the inhabitants of the widely separated ninety-nine castles in the vicinity, who were being maltreated by the Saracens and other barbarians. In memory of this, it now boasts ninety-nine of everything. There are ninety-nine *rioni* or administrative sections, each representing one of the old castles; ninety-nine piazzas; ninety-nine fountains; ninety-nine churches. At two o'clock every night—the guide-book claims—the bell of the central church is struck ninety-nine times. I did not hear this, but I sat by the famous fountain of the ninety-nine heads. The guide-book also enumerates the list of conquerors Aquila has known, finishing on a characteristic lofty note: "Byzantines, Langobards, Goths, Normans, Saracens, Guelphs, Ghibellines, Hohenstaufens, Angevins, Spaniards—and now, English and Americans! We have known them all. We can look the future in the face!"

And this is no vain boast. A glance at the history book shows that, even among the cities of this much-buffeted peninsula, Aquila stands high for revolution, earthquake, cataclysm and sudden death. In modern times alone it has had at least twenty changes of régime. A Ghibelline city in the twelfth century, it suddenly went over to the Guelphs in the thirteenth, and was entirely destroyed by Manfred in 1268. A little later, Charles of Anjou rebuilt it. In 1423 a *condottiere* called Braccio da Montone, who had been promised the city as a present by Joan II of Naples, unable to get it without knocking it down, did so again. Joan and her successors then rebuilt it. After that, what man had not destroyed, Nature did—with earthquakes in 1461 and 1471. In 1493 the plague possessed it, decimating the population. In 1503 the Spaniards, appearing on the Italian scene for the first time, invested it and knocked down anything that was left standing. In 1703 the most terrible earthquake of all killed 6,000 people.

"After this", says the guide-book, "it arose with quite another aspect."

The final stage of our journey to this historic place was made along the *via Sabina*, through the sober countryside of the valley of the Aterno River, only enlivened from time to time on the dusty road by a silvery stream that crossed beneath or, in the well-tilled fields, by the grey-green of olives still in bloom. At last we saw, rising in the distance, the finger of a campanile, about whose base clustered those arches, domes and spires which are seldom long absent from the traveller's gaze as he journeys down the land of Italy.

The sun was low, but the sky was still blue and clear when we entered the city of Frederick II. The *sobborgo* or suburb near the famous fountain had an attractive air of rusticity for a capital—the walls embowered among their own vines and fig-trees, the roofs pictur-esque with pigeons; in the courtyards were wine-presses, threshing-floors and other signs of rural life. By the fountain with the ninety-nine heads, some girls, barefooted, awaited their turn to fill pots and jugs. They were lightly clad although the evening was cool, some with bracelets gleaming on their wrists, others with brown shawls, all worthy of the honour of the local picture postcard.

I had read somewhere that the young peasant girls of these parts live in almost patriarchal seclusion, never looking at strangers, averting their eyes at your glance, blushing, being as timid as gazelles. But the slow movement with which one of these now examined me abstractedly, lowered her eyelids and veiled her eyes might have been that of Carmen herself.

We made our way up the hill and came to a market-place crammed with canvas-coloured booths, stalls, people, horses, mules, carts, among which moved a troop of pilgrims carrying bundles, armed with huge green, brown and black umbrellas. It was a Sunday; and from an improvised outdoor pulpit a priest was addressing this variegated and mobile congregation. For, as is so often the case in Italy, the spiritual and secular pursuits of the listeners intermingled. Some were listening attentively; some eating melon at fly-blown stalls; some sitting back at café tables, or buying from men with collapsible trays and all those other itinerant persons of an Italian piazza. *In Italia la vita si fa in piazza!* All, however, appeared more or less interested in the sermon which was about Purgatory. The priest was exhorting the congregation to piety— for in these days of Holy Year, he said, the force of prayer is greater. He spoke emphatically, with a sonorous voice, sometimes, I thought, a trifle pompously.

He appeared not at all disturbed by the fluctuations in his auditorium. Even when a large lorry appeared and backed right across the piazza, emitting bangs and sparks and clouds of black smoke, he ignored it, only stopping momentarily when it was right beneath the pulpit and he could not hear his own voice—and then continuing with unabated vehemence.

It was in Aquila that I was first made aware of the unstable soil of central Italy, its predisposition to earthquake, landslide and volcano. I had read in the guide-book that the inhabitants of Aquila had, as a result of so many earthquakes, made a vow to their patron saint, Emidio, that they would renounce the first two weeks of their annual carnival if they could be spared them a little. Although the prayer does not seem to have been answered, the carnival still starts on the 17th February instead of the 3rd February.

Not long before our arrival, a considerable tremor had shaken the city. And in the barber's shop on my first morning, I met a man who, on my asking what measures were taken against them, gave me a most graphic description of earthquakes in these parts. (I should add that this is most unusual, for the Aquilans, like all people suffering from a particular affliction, have an inferiority complex about it. They do not like talking about earthquakes, particularly to visitors.) But this man came from Naples, which perhaps accounted for his readiness. He was an immense, tall fellow, with moustaches and an assumed military air—clearly the chief *ciarlone*, or chatterer, of the place.

"Earthquakes!" he said proudly. "I have known four in my time. The first, as a child, being the terrible one of 1901."

I asked him to describe this. Being an Italian and a philosopher however, he prefaced his gruesome description with one or two metaphysical observations about natural phenomena in general.

"Although they are the most fearful signs of the power of Nature," he said, "I cannot condemn them in our modern world, which is doing all it can to create artificial earthquakes. With atom bombs. And then invent antidotes for them! Let us never forget that whatever we do, however clever we may think we are, we can never defend ourselves against Nature, *the all-powerful Goddess!"*

"Modern science," I said, "may indeed create artificial earthquakes. But it also affords us means of building strongly. To resist natural ones."

"A fig for your modern science!" he said. "The scientists to-day are so many sorcerers' apprentices. With their pacificism and their pious hopes that what they have invented will not damage the world! Why, they have unloosed all the devils in creation!" And then he went on to draw a truly terrifying picture of the future, forgetting all about the earthquake for the moment, addressing me as if I, as an Anglo-Saxon, was personally responsible for nuclear physics.

"All of us," he said bitterly, *"all of us* will be swallowed up in incandescent gases and projected with immense explosions into space, pulverised into a million million atoms. Perhaps in the disasters before us we shall not *all* die immediately. But those who remain will have to start everything from nothing again. Like the savages in the mists of history. . . ."

He continued like this for some time, before I could get him to describe any of the natural disasters he had known. But when he did, I began to understand his terrible fatalism. When you are born and bred in a land where the very ground beneath your feet is unstable, where you lose your innate belief in the "sure and firm-set earth" (which we northerners all take for granted), you must have a certain hesitancy, a lack of confidence in the future. The graphic description he now gave, I have tried to set down exactly.

"The summer of 1901 had," he said, "been one of the hottest known to man. The ground was drier than it had ever been before. Then followed an autumn and winter which were more rainy than all the previous ones. From October till the end of January, rain never stopped falling. In veritable cataracts. The valleys became marshes and the hillsides ran with mud. But then, in the last days of January, the weather turned to fine again.

"On the 5th of February a fine day dawned. The temperature was a little higher than usual. Only one or two clouds lay above, in a blue sky. All Nature, at the approach of spring, seemed at last to take on her beauty under a radiant sun. Nothing foretold the disaster. Only the animals, it is said, gave signs of inexplicable emotion. The hens fluttered in the courtyards, as if trying to escape. Horses pawed the ground with a sort of anguished excitement, stiffened their ears and neighed. Most extraordinary of all, the cows spread their four legs apart, as if trying to set themselves more firmly on the ground. Cats and dogs fled from the houses and slunk in the streets. Suddenly, just before 12.30, a sound more violent than thunder was heard in the ground beneath. Followed some seconds after by a convulsion, a splitting of the earth such as has never been known before or since. It lasted just thirty seconds. But in that short time, not a house was left standing within a radius of a hundred miles. And 30,000 dead lay buried under the ruins. Eyewitnesses say that in the country great undulations like waves of the sea took place. And peasants disappeared in vast fissures, which opened beneath their feet. And shut up again almost as quickly on their victims. In the villages fires broke out, for all the hearths were alight for the midday meal.

"Such, my English friend," he finished, pointing his finger at me accusingly, "is the land you are now in. You say you are interested in earthquakes. Well, if you stay here a few weeks more, you may be lucky enough to have one yourself. For these things generally occur in cycles. And we have already had one or two minor oscillations this year. Stay and see!"

I thanked him for this description; which was quite

D

graphic enough for me not to wish "to be lucky enough
to have one myself".

And the man was right. For two months later, an
earthquake *did* take place in the neighbourhood of
Aquila, killing fifty-three people.

The barber's shop where this conversation took
place is one of the great meeting-places of male society
in Italy. Here on the benches, opportunities for such
conversation are unlimited. And as every Italian has
his own theory about life and death and the meaning
of existence, many were the views I heard expressed
during my week in Aquila, in this little fly-free arbour
with its electric fans and cigar smoke, off the Piazza
Regina Margherita. It was no ordinary establishment—
but the *Albergo Diurno*, where people could have their
nails manicured, hair waved, shoes shined, clothes
pressed; they could leave luggage and make telephone
calls. Here I had my hair cut, or rather shorn, by a
lightning barber. I had no time to read, bewildered,
following his twitching hands, watching them in the
glass as one might a ping-pong match. He did not use
those fearsome clippers, but did it in the old-fashioned
way, with scissors. They must have twitched several
thousand times during my five minutes in the chair.

It all reminded me of that barber's shop described
in *Romola*, with something too of that lingering dignity
which still remains in the Italian barber, owing perhaps
to this ancient profession of surgeon.

CHAPTER SIX

Aquila

"AQUILA STRONG AND kind!" sings the guide-book. "One of the most picturesque regions of Italy. With wild mountain gorges, vast panoramas, solitary monasteries, ancient costumes and turreted towns set on hill-tops like fortresses. A land where flock and shepherd continue their age-old passage from plain to hill and hill to plain. Here has been conserved the rhythm of pastoral life. And the visitor, if he finds the hotal arrangements a trifle deficient, will agree that the cordial hospitality of the inhabitants is a sufficient recompense. These hotel deficiencies, incidentally, are rapidly being eliminated. . . ."

The last sentence clearly refers to the late régime (when the book was written), which has taken full advantage of this earthquake-ridden town to indulge its whim for heavy, monumental architecture. In spite of this however, the "hotel deficiencies" are still appreciable.

I learnt here that there are two things which the experienced traveller must always carry with him for his hotel in wayside Italy—a cork, and an electric-light bulb. On entering his bedroom he will fit the cork where there should be a plug in the wash-basin; or his rest will be continually disturbed by unpalatable odours. For an Italian hotel wash-basin, if uncorked, talks; you can hear it gurgling, commenting all night. The electric-light bulb will be needed because the light provided will be too dim for reading, just enough to undress by.

When I asked the hotel manageress in this Aquila

hotel for a cork, she became most suspicious, convinced that I was about to use it for some illicit purpose. Her suspicion turned to anger when she found that I had inserted a 60-watt bulb in the place of the watery glow provided. A charge for extra electricity would be made!

Such sordidness, together with the wretched bed-room I had been allotted on the top floor, irritated me. I went downstairs. "*Signora*," I said, "this is Holy Year, is it not?"

"*Si, signore!*"

"And you are a Christian?"

"*Si, signore!*"

"And you wish American tourists to come to your hotel?"

"*Si, si, si, signore!*"

"Well, I am a journalist, and I write for a paper called the *Catholic Holiday Tourist*, with a *vast* circulation in the United States. And in it I shall say that your hotel is the lousiest, most unswept, insalubrious, bed-bug-ridden plague-spot I have ever come across in all my long and painful wandering in Italy."

Such a method is extreme. These words might well have had the reverse effect from that intended. And I was quite prepared to be thrown out on the spot. But the effect this time was excellent. Within an hour, I was installed in another room, on the first floor, quite well illuminated; in which a cork was later brought to me on a plate for which I was afterwards charged on the bill, 50 *lire*. (Yet I have been charged for an aspirin in an Italian hotel.)

What traveller after traveller in this land has complained about for the last 600 years is still unfortunately true. The charming Italians spoil themselves by their grasping nature and their commercial dishonesty. You must ask the price of the least item before accepting it, in goods and services—or you will be swindled. When by chance, at a café table, in conversation with a friend or engrossed in a newspaper, you neglect to ask the price before ordering a glass of something or other, you will be infuriated by the waiter, who will blandly ask 50 per cent. more than he did the day before—when you asked the price.

You are about to revile the smiling villain, when you suddenly recollect and realise you cannot. A race that has been oppressed and robbed by foreigners and foreign rule for so many centuries must be forgiven much. He smiles at you as only an Italian can, whether you curse him or cajole him—and you suddenly realise how much you love this warm-hearted, quick-fingered, dishonest race.

I have only met one man who claimed he had never been swindled in Italy; a Swiss. I asked him how he carried out this superhuman feat, and he told me that he was always *extrêmement méticuleux*. He watched his drinks being mixed; he refused to pay tips included in the bill; he gave them personally to the staff (even going into the kitchen). He kept an account book of all he spent and how he spent it, in each town—to compare prices.

"First of all in a new town," he said, "I always ask if there is an inn with a German landlord. It is sure to be cleaner and more honest. Then I check the bill. And always, you know, I find an error in it. And always, finally, they admit that error."

Such vigilance however, seems to me to make meals scarcely worth eating.

But everyone in Italy to-day is poor; all are interested in where their money goes. There are two classes, however—those *aggressively* interested, and those *defensively* interested, in it. The problem is to keep to the second class. So far, on my journey, I had managed to do so. But I wondered how long it would be before I joined the majority.

Aquila, being like most central Italian cities on a hill, is almost entirely deprived of level streets, and one climbs and descends everywhere. The highest mountains of the peninsula, many of them like the Gran Sasso snow-clad, surround it, giving the human being a feeling of insignificance unfamiliar to the dweller of the plain, where, as in a city like London or Milan, man dominates Nature, obliterates it even. In the Aquilan landscape, a New York skyscraper would still be a secondary element.

In no other part of Italy can one say therefore that the life of the people has been so influenced by geography. Seventy per cent. of the Abruzzi, the guide-book claims, is composed of mountains; and intercourse between the villages or unification of the peoples who inhabit the valleys, has always been difficult. The Equines, Marsians, Pelignians, Vestinians of pre-Roman times were always foreigners to one another; as they still are in many respects. Other civilisations did not penetrate here. The barbarians of Calabria knew the civilisation of Greece, thanks to their sea-line; those of the Adriatic, that of Byzantium. But these people, only 100 miles from Rome, remained remote, hostile even to one another, long after Rome had extended her Empire to the Thames and the Euphrates.

Communications with Rome are transversal, across the mountains, and have always been much harder than those with the more distant north and south—even in modern times. It was enough in the recent wars for the two main bridges on the Avezzano-Tivoli road to be destroyed and Aquila was cut off from Rome as completely as it was in the days of Frederick II.

The same physical causes were later responsible for the tardy penetration of other civilisations; the Renaissance; the Jacobinism the Napoleonic armies brought with them; even the *Risorgimento* itself. The architecture tells the same tale. The only Renaissance building

of any note is San Bernadino in Aquila. Elsewhere
Gothic and Romanesque abound. This perhaps explains
why Aquila, although belonging geographically to
central Italy, has always followed the history of the
south, of the Two Sicilies. With the exception of brief
periods of French, Austrian and Pontifical rule, Aquila
has always been under whoever was oppressing Naples
at the time—the Normans of Capua, the Normans of
Puglia, the Normans of Sicily, the Swabians, the
Aragonese, the Castilians, and finally—the Spanish
Bourbons installed by the distant court of Madrid.

This last rule, the longest and most benumbing of
all, is still written largely on the ground to the east of
the town, where the great Spanish Viceroy's castle
rears itself. Its intention—the oppression of the local
inhabitants—is written as clearly in its vast mole as
in the inscription placed ostentatiously over the draw-
bridge—*Ad reprimendam contumaciam Aquilinorum.*
That such words have not been effaced by the modern
Aquilans—will even be shown you with pride—surely
tells more about them than any history book. For
nearly 200 years this moated castle, looking out on to
the magnificent panorama of the Gran Sasso range,
the distant Maiella, the groups of the Velino and the
Sirente mountains, made any *contumacia* on their part
impossible.

Its gigantic ramparts, the sombre russet tone with
which time has endowed it, the wild plants that grow
in the moat, its position dominating the town—all
these together produce an unforgettable feeling of the
force, brutal but spent, of that Spanish domination
which after the Battle of Pavia, put an end to
indigenous Italian civilisation. Think of the tragic
history of the Kingdom of Naples; modify it, or
intensify it, by neglect—and you have the history of
Aquila.

Centuries passed and all the rulers of this land were

strangers to the Aquilans. Romans and Goths, Lombards and Franks, Germans and Spaniards, they all
came and went, with their own laws and customs
which were set up and then disappeared, all of them
arbitrary and accidental in the eyes of the people.
Isolated in these mountains, the Aquilans learnt
instead a resignation strongly tinged with cynicism,
content to keep their cattle and pursue their activities,
glad when nobody meddled. Is it surprising, then,
that these people, unlike those of other parts of Italy—
most of whom display the current European vice of
history-wagging—should not have bothered to efface
those impertinent words on the castle?

Venetians, Milanese, even Neapolitans will try to
prove to you that they have, at some time or other,
had a victory. The Aquilans have never known anything but service in other people's armies. Even during
the recent wars they found themselves enlisted to fight
for Germans, English, Americans, Russians, or whoever happened to be occupying their land at the time.
They fought in places as far away as the Caucasus and
the Malay Peninsula. Some have yet to return from
those heroic expeditions.

That Conquerors have only recently left Aquila is
clear from another, much more modern inscription,
which the natives have also not bothered to efface.
I found it in a dirty side-street, still visible in black
and white; the large English letters, THIS STREET IS
OUT OF BOUNDS TO ALLIED TROOPS.

I wandered down it and immediately understood why it had been posted. It was clearly not
a place where our generals would have liked to see
their "well-disciplined troops" disporting themselves
five years ago. A "red-light" district. Pails of refuse
stood in the gutters, mangy cats and dogs slunk about;
and a pair of sarcastic prostitutes hung blowsily out of
a window, making obscene remarks as I passed. Some

soldiers were washing at a pump, and one of them was talking to a woman who leant against the door-post of a house, half-obscured by the heavy bead curtain which takes the place of a door in the south. She also belonged to the oldest profession. That she was speaking forcibly, I could see from her expression and gestures. It evidently infuriated the soldier, for he suddenly let out a kick at her. She squealed and retired behind the curtain. He followed and, judging from the noises I heard within, appeared to be giving her a good hiding—when suddenly, as in those nocturnal rambles of cats on roof-tops, the wailing and scrapping ceased; and was replaced by complete silence! A feeling of unexpected tenderness pervaded the fœtid air. Venus had replaced Mars. And the other soldiers laughed coarsely. . . .

I heard of another, even more picturesque case of foreign interference in these parts—from an English friend who had also been travelling in the Abruzzi. He told me he was talking to a small and extremely dirty man in the street one day, about some trivial topographical direction, when the man, disapproving of his accent, suddenly broke into fluent German. My friend said he knew no German. Whereupon the little man began to speak Russian. My friend knew a little Russian and, as such a command of languages in so unprepossessing a person fascinated him, he asked where he had learnt it. The Aquilan replied that the recent wars were responsible. In the autumn of 1941 he had set out with Adolf Hitler on the conquest of Russia. This adventure had, as his appearance showed, brought him small profit; on my friend asking him his present occupation, he held out his hat.

They then went into a nearby café, where, over two small cups of very black coffee, the Italian told him about his time in Russia. All, it appeared, had gone well to begin with. He had advanced superbly and entered various cities. But on the way back in winter the poor fellow, half frozen, fell into the hands of the peasants of Orel. They shut him up for the night in an open meat-coop and the next morning, taking him down to the river in which a hole had been made in the ice, invited him to dive into it. He was unable to agree to this request, which in any case, he only understood from their gestures; and so he prayed them to allow him to continue his way back to Aquila unhindered.

But the peasants of Orel, probably through ignorance that there was such a place as Aquila, continued to suggest the course beneath the ice. And they were stimulating him to it with hand and foot when suddenly, to his inexpressible joy, a sound of bells announced the arrival of a sleigh. In it sat a fat and jolly Commissar.

"What the devil are you up to?" he said.

"We are drowning a German, Your Excellency," said the peasants.

"Splendid!" said the Commissar. And he ordered the sleigh to continue.

"*Signore, mi aiuti per l'amor di Dio!*" cried the Italian.

"Ah," said the Commissar, turning, "this is no German. He is an Italian. He is probably a musician." And to the Italian he said: "You came against Kiev accompanied by people talking twenty different languages. You set fire to Pimsk, Bomsk and Tomsk. You villain! Can you play the piano? I require someone to give my daughter lessons."

In these circumstances, said the Aquilan, he had no alternative but to say, yes; although he could not play the piano. Whereupon, the Commissar drove him away in his sleigh and took him home, where he was fed and warmed. He was then taken before a piano and the daughter. "Here, little one," said the Commissar, "is your piano teacher. He will also teach you

Italian. Play!" he commanded the Italian. "Show your art!"

"I strummed on the keys a little," said the Aquilan to my friend. "What else could I do? I thought he would have me hanged immediately. Instead, to my unspeakable surprise, the Commissar hit me on the shoulders with great goodwill. 'Good! Good!' he cried. 'I can see you are a musician. But you are tired. Now go up and sleep.'

"And that was how," said the Aquilan, "I learnt Russian. I spent three years teaching her Italian, and working on the farm. And then I came home with the first train of prisoners of war."

"And how about the piano lessons?" said my friend.

"I taught her to sing instead."

In any other country one would have expressed surprise at this—incredulity even. But not in Italy.

CHAPTER SEVEN

An Amphitheatre

THERE IS PROBABLY no monument that symbolises civilisation better than the amphitheatre. If the Greeks gave us the theatre, where the passions depicted were human, the Romans gave us the amphitheatre, where they were bestial. Those terrible names, Nero, Decius, Domitian, evoke immediately the spectacle of that walled ellipse which arose wherever the Roman armies triumphed; of which the Coliseum is the supreme example.

Impressive as that amphitheatre is, however, it is less moving, I find, than other more dilapidated examples scattered throughout the western Empire; perhaps because it has been repaired and renovated so often, equipped with guides and turnstiles and all the panoply of the tourist shrine. The passage of time is less clearly written on it than upon those hulks over which the ivy, the myrtle and the asphodel have climbed. Sometimes, in the extreme cases, as at Fréjus or Dorchester, not a brick remains—a grassy hollow in the ground, a dell, whose elliptical shape alone tells that once a consul sat here among the columns and marbles and graded tiers. At other places, as at Arles or Pozzuoli, the site is better preserved; the brickwork remains, broken but identifiable. Human beings have always lived here and encroaching Nature has been kept away.

The amphitheatre of Amiternum, an extinct Latin city five miles north of Aquila, really belongs to the first category, although the outer walls are still standing. But earth had piled up around them and the marbles have long been stolen by succeeding civilisations. Grass and moss grow in their crevices, and the long stems of wild plants sway at their base under the *scirocco*. That human beings seldom come out here because the place is remote in its natural, even more majestic amphitheatre of the Apennines, is attested by the swallows who have made their nests in the lowest part of the walls. The centre has become simply an oval field into which goats occasionally wander, where all manner of wild flowers grow and where the cricket sings his amorous, anacreontic song all day— all that remains of the Sabine city of Amiternum, where Sallust was born 2,000 years ago.

One morning in June we came out from Aquila, and I walked about among the flora and fauna of the amphitheatre. At first sight, and from a distance, these walls seem simply lumps of calcined rock which might just as well be on the moon. Closer acquaintance however, reveals that among them spring thousands of leaves and flowers, in the cracks where immemorial dirt has gathered, with those long, fleshy leaves and that rich quality of foliage found in desert plants which must form a reservoir of moisture in a' week, for the rest of the year. I climbed to the top of the walls and looked down where the debris of column and arch rise up among the bushes and cypresses, and tried to imagine its appearance 2,000 years ago. In this wonderful land of Italy there is not a corner, not a strip, however hidden or isolated, which does not evoke some memory of departed greatness.

An ingenious German, Friedlander, has composed a table of all the amphitheatres in the world, with their exact dimensions and seating accommodation. The biggest is the Coliseum, which housed 50,000; the smallest that of Ventimiglia, with 4,000. This one at Amiternum must have been about halfway between; but owing to the greatness of the local Flavian house

(Vespasian came from Rieti) of considerable importance. The guide-book—with a scientific impartiality quite Italian—then mentions that there is in England, outside London, an amphitheatre which holds an even greater number than any in the Italian peninsula—Wembley! It was odd, looking down on this grassy arena, once sanded and level, populated by gladiators and beasts, to think that if Amiternum were still alive to-day, a football match *all' Inglese* between Aquila and Sulmona would probably be in progress before my eyes.

While walking round the arena I met a viper. It was my first and, I am thankful to say, my only meeting with the poisonous snakes of Southern Italy. It lay in my path and I knew its species; for instead of wriggling away, as do all the larger, non-poisonous snakes at a man's approach, it turned, raised its head and, after we had examined one another for a while, emitted the well-known, venomous hiss. Then, slowly, it started moving towards me.

I am always amazed at the sense these insignificant-looking little reptiles have of their own deadliness. They know that they can kill. I immediately spread my coat in front and began to retreat, having heard that the viper will jump, like a spring, for the eyes. Still hissing, it advanced, and I was beginning to wonder how long before it struck—for as I accelerated backwards, it increased its speed—when, without warning, it suddenly darted off to the side, under a bush.

I told Masceri about this later. He said, "*Signorino*, if it had bitten you, you would have had an hour to live. Unless you had an antidote. My uncle lived only half an hour. But you are young. You would have resisted the poison better."

"And what," I asked, "would you have done during that hour? Rushed to Aquila for the antidote or a doctor, I hope?"

"A doctor! There is no such thing in this land."
He pointed forlornly around. "No, all we could have
done would have been to wait and see which was the
stronger, you or the poison. We should have known in
an hour."

A crowded hour!

Masceri, I had discovered, knew quite a lot about
the local fauna and flora. Here, in this arena with its
quantities of wild flowers, his knowledge was of great
value. When he saw that they interested me, he was
for ever pointing them out. "Look!" he would cry.
"Stinkwort!" (or its Italian equivalent). And I would
bend down among what seemed to me the usual
assortment of daisies and dandelions and examine the
flower carefully, and try to remember its exact shape
and petal formation. And then a little further on, he
would cry, "Look! Love-in-a-meadow!" And on
examination, I would find almost no difference between
stinkwort and love-in-a-meadow.

That wonderful botanical domain, even in England,
full of its beautiful Elizabethan names, has always been
closed to me. I can never remember the name of a cultivated flower, let alone a wild one; although with trees and
shrubs I am more familiar. In spite of all my visits as a
child to Kew Gardens with my mother, where elementary
things like primroses and pansies and hollyhocks were
pointed out, I never improved. But on this Sabine
journey, with the information of Masceri, who had
his own names for them, and Foligno's excellent book,
La Flora selvatica d'Italia, I learned to distinguish
the lentisk, the yellow camomile, the teasel with its
greyish beard, the fuchsia, the woodbine, the aromatic
mint and the caprieul—a sea of wild flowers ravishing
sight and smell, leaving perhaps a more lasting impression of Italy than all the books.

In the typical Roman amphitheatre, as here at

Amiternum, the arena was usually above a substratum, where the wild beasts, the gladiators, criminals and Christians were housed. The seats of the spectators were numbered and reserved, just as to-day. Tickets of clay have been found in the surrounding fields of Amiternum. The spectators were seated in social orders. In the lowest tiers, the *podium*, were the nobles and State officials; above them, the wealthy and commercial classes; then the *plebs*; and at the very top, in accordance with the orders of Augustus, the women.

The man who seems to have enjoyed these amphitheatres most was, as one might imagine, Nero, who insisted that the gladiators should be beautifully dressed; that while they fought, a heavy blue cloth studded with silver stars should be hoisted above them, to protect them from the sun. He also replaced the sand on the floor by cinnamon powder.

Historians say that the amphitheatre, as a Latin institution, dates from as early as 263 B.C., and was connected with the funeral service of some distinguished citizen. It appears that a magistrate was always in charge of this service, and that he was expected to give some grandiose entertainment at it, such as a gladiatorial display. This was later extended to the killing of wild beasts and the execution of criminals and Christians. The magistrate naturally wished to make a name for himself; and the spot where these funereal amusements took place, at first an open space, gradually became more elaborate, with walls and decorations, finally evolving into the amphitheatre of classical times.

Christians were killed as simple criminals to begin with; but that particular sport really marked the beginning of the end of the amphitheatre. For in A.D. 326 Constantine published an edict that Christians, hitherto condemned with other criminals *ad bestias*, should henceforth be condemned *ad metalla*, and work in the mines. Under Theodoric, the schools of gladiators were closed; it must have seemed like the Puritan closing of the theatres in our own country. And in A.D. 681 Justinian put an end to the amphitheatre as a scene of entertainment altogether, by forbidding any kind of amusement in it. All that remained for it, then, was to become a fortress or a convent in the Dark Ages, degenerating into a quarry for building materials in feudal times; a museum in the Renaissance; and finally, as to-day, into a place where the spider spins her web and where, in the innumerable crevices, the scorpion finds a refuge.

Outside this amphitheatre is a line of excavations, a ditch recently started by the Department of Archæology, bordered by all the objects the earth has, after nearly 2,000 years, begun to give up—architraves, statues, tombs, rostral columns—truly the land of "thou broken column with a buried base". A row of cypresses lines one side, and down this avenue of excavations I walked at midday in the sun. Apart from the ubiquitous lizards and a solitary workman, I was alone. This man, who was eating his lunch under a tree, was unearthing Roman statues and Roman skulls. And I suddenly felt as if I were present at the unwinding of some sort of mummy, concealed in its shroud since history began.

In a nearby field, sheep wandered, tended by a disconsolate shepherd. Man and beast seemed as much a part of the landscape as the columns and marbles beside them, their movements now much as they must have been 2,000 years ago. And as I heard them bleating in the distance, I reflected that the lowly word "bleat" (*balare* in Latin) is the origin of the noble word *Palatine*, on which Augustus built his palace in Rome—now enriched with all its modern derivations, *palatial*, *paladin*, *palazzo*! For it refers to

E

the sheep, the *bleaters* which wandered about that classic Roman mount in prehistoric times.

Their shepherd too is considered about the lowest form of human life, the human equivalent of his charge, the *balantes*. And yet here he is, listening day by day as he chews a blade of grass beneath a tree to the eternal bleat, the royal, the *palatial* bleat, of the animals whose wool created the wealth and civilisations of Rome and England; and which will presumably, long after the modern ones have raved and rocketed themselves out, create the stuff of countless civilisations to come.

CHAPTER EIGHT

Three Villages

ANYONE WHO HAS visited the Five Towns area of England will remember the sudden darkening of the horizon as the train leaves the verdant countryside of Shropshire and enters the valley of the Trent. In that vale are concentrated most of the potteries of England, beneath a canopy of greenish-yellow smoke. Not a blade of grass is to be seen. Nature is effaced in an atmosphere that is unique in its theatrical effects. Bottle-shaped factories belch forth orange-coloured smoke and flame; the air breathes chemistry. The very people themselves in this sad half-light seem like waxworks. It is a relief to come out an hour later into the sunlight of Cheshire.

The Abruzzi counterpart to this, the village of Castelli, lies in one of the central Apennine valleys. It is approached from the east through surrounding foothills, wave upon wave of them, stretching gently away to the horizon and the Adriatic. The valley is rich with the alluvial soil brought down by the rivers, so that the area is marvellously fertile. Not an inch of the cornucopia is left uncultivated. Figs, peaches, pears and grapes abound. Five crops of tomatoes a year are produced. The pomegranate, with its appearance of an overripe orange—until one nears it and sees the serrated fringe of green—catches the eye from afar. Above all this rise the thin chimneys of the Castelli pottery works.

It was here, in the early days of the Renaissance, that the fertile river clay was discovered to have yet another quality. It could be easily manipulated by hand, yet it hardened suddenly; and could thus be adapted to the uses to which della Robbia and his brothers in Florence were putting the clay of the Val d'Arno, from which had sprung the greatest china of the Renaissance.

In one of these factories I spoke to an elderly potter. The respect which he showed for our Five Towns china was gratifying. "We can never compete with Wedgwood craftmanship," he said. "The English are the finest potters in the world"—praise which I had hardly expected in the land of Majolica. He then. showed me round the factory. And here I understood the meaning of the word "craftsman." The training they undergo lasts a lifetime. As we went from room to room their age increased. In the first, were young men and women, just apprenticed, from sixteen to twenty-five, occupied with the simplest forms, pots, pans, round bowls and vases. Then, as the work became more delicate, the age increased. And in the last room of all, where the most intricate forms were created, sat the experts at the wheels, wizened little old men and women, heavily bespectacled, their eyesight impaired by decades of squinting at the lumps of clay before them; but which, under the touch of a finger or a thumbnail cunningly applied to the whirling mass, began to assume the most imaginative forms.

The Castelli school of ceramics was founded by Renzo and Polidoro di Lanciano in the fourteenth century. Since then a series of dynastic pottery families have flourished in this village, of which the most famous is that of the Grue, in the eighteenth century. So distinguished did this family of potters become that at the *Risorgimento* the title of *Royal School of Art, Francesco Grue*, was granted to the factory. An unending quantity of different objects have issued from this little building for nearly 600 years—tiles for floors, candelabras, lanterns, picture-frames, tobacco boxes, even an encaustic organ. These were some of the things I saw. The subjects treated are sacred, historical and allegorical, with a number of battles, hunts and passions—those scenes of violence beloved by the Italian, whether on the plate of his dinner service or on the operatic stage of Verdi before him.

I came out to this village from Aquila by train. It would have been too difficult to cross the mountains on foot, so I left Masceri and Pepe to idle in the capital for forty-eight hours, while I studied the art of Italian ceramics.

On the journey I found myself in the same carriage as a father, mother and daughter who had just returned from America to visit this village of Castelli, their *patria*. The man had been a potter there, he said—as had been his father and grandfather. But he had abandoned it twenty-six years ago to become a farmer in Dallas! Here he must have prospered. His spruce clothes, variegated tie and rimless spectacles belied his peasant face. And when I tried to get him to talk Italian, even I could appreciate its rustiness. He lent me the *New Haven Gazette*, and I offered him in return my *Corriere della Sera*—which he politely refused.

All three of these *Americanos* had an air of considerable well-being; and the thin, pursed lips of the daughter, although silent, spoke clearly of that continent. She was a lissom creature of about twenty-one, clad in Hollywood style, with a large floppy white hat—by some fluke of Nature, fair and blue-eyed, so that I would have instinctively classed her as Anglo-Saxon. But there was no doubt about Mamma's origin. The liquid, coal-black eyes were entirely Italian and she talked continuously and excitedly about the homecoming. Father was less enthusiastic. And for the daughter, the whole thing was obviously a bore. She spoke seldom; and when she did, replied to her mother's excited Italian shortly, in mono-syllabic English, gazing abstractedly out of the window all the time, her mind far away—fixed, no doubt, on some curly-headed giant in Texas.

They got out at a little halt just before Castelli, with chickens wandering aimlessly about a weed-encrusted platform, and carried their garish suitcases, covered with hotel labels, to I know not what hovel. For on the platform I saw the "uncle" they had been talking about, waiting to receive them. He looked like a Sicilian bandit; with a huge black hat, a handle-bar moustache, and mahogany skin. *Zio Beppo!*

The village of San Pio which we visited the following day on our journey to Sulmona was the birthplace of Pontius Pilate. It is about as different from Castelli as the Five Towns are—but in a different way. If Hercules, on his arrival in Italy to kill the giant Cacus, had seen this grubby little village on a hill, he would have certainly dedicated one of his labours to cleaning it up. Nowhere perhaps have I been more conscious of that belief, deeply founded in rural Italy, that any-thing can be deposited in the street—and by extension, that it can also be deposited in the house. The narrow streets with their uneven, polygonal *pavé* were strewn with rubbish and excrement in which pigs were wallowing. Huge, loathsome flies buzzed about. The floors inside the houses were of beaten earth covered with pumpkin husks, orange peel and bits of water-melon. On this natural mosaic frolicked ragged youths, their faces burned by the sun, their hair long, raven-black, clotted. Sometimes they attacked one another, sometimes the goats that shared their life. A rustic tranquillity, a total lack even of commercial activity, gave the place a feeling of the Dark Ages. Was this the punishment, this lack of self-respect—a

Christian might well ask—for the place that bore and nourished Pontius Pilate?

In Italian wayside villages you will frequently see small children running about naked, or at least with nothing on their lower quarters, so that the requirements of Nature can be met directly, without giving the trouble and expense to Mamma of washing the garments of the less accurate. But I had never seen a mother, as I did here, minister to her child in the following fashion: She turned it so that it faced her; put its head firmly between her legs; clamped them; and then, ignoring the infant's squeals, proceeded to pummel its naked quarters. When, with much effort and surrounded by the indulgent smiles of other women, it had produced what was required, she picked up a handy bit of newspaper and, for some reason of inexplicable delicacy, wiped it—afterwards throwing the paper back into the street. She then sat down before her house again and took up her knitting and chatting, while the child went on playing in the filth.

Why, I have often wondered, are such contrasts to be found in Italy; the abundance of the countryside and the squalor of its villages? This suave Pelignian vale—and the cynical slatternliness of its inhabitants? Walking up these slopes, I had been struck by the trees of this land—almonds, chestnuts, pomegranates, figs—all of which succeed one another throughout the year, so that no sooner has one been harvested before another appears with a new production, while a third is showing its buds. Surrounded by such abundance, why should these people be poor? Why, in this *Saturnia tellus*, does such misery prevail?

The answer seems to be that all these fruits and wines and other products are sold for a paltry sum, while the greater proportion of them go by the *métayage* system to the absentee landlord. That scourge of Italy, the *latifundia*, which the Gracchi tried to abolish

2,000 years ago (just as De Gaspari does to-day), still flourishes. It must be endemic to the peninsula. Were it not for the *granturco* and maize, from which the peasants make their eternal *polenta*, they would starve, for they cannot afford to buy the other crops they harvest.

At this time of the year the fields were all yellow with sheaves of this *granturco*; even the windows of the village houses, from which they hung drying in the sun. When these sheaves are dry, they are reduced to pulp, then spread out on a flat stone and afterwards cooked over a brazier. All the family sit around the fire and swallow it hot, seasoned with a little olive oil if they can afford it, more often with vile-tasting chicory or those other substitutes for green vegetables which distinguish the *cucina* of Southern Italy.

Of San Pio's greatest citizen I discovered only this— over a glass of wine in a darkened booth, whose walls were black with the smoke of years, so that even the painting of the Madonna, illuminated by a swinging oil-lamp, seemed one with its background. My informant told me in this penumbra, that after the death of Christ, Pontius Pilate was recalled to Rome to give an account of his misdoings. Here he immediately committed suicide. His body was thrown into the Tiber and carried out to sea; it floated to the Rhone, up which it went, until it arrived at the Swiss lakes. (This was to take it as far away as possible from Italy and San Pio, both of whom disowned it.) Here, on reaching Lucerne, it suddenly sank, making a tremendous noise, near the mountain now called Pilatus. He added that Pontius Pilate and his wife have since been canonised by the Coptic Church.

I learnt later that the man who told me all this was the sacristan.

The third village near Aquila we visited before continuing our journey to Sulmona was Fossa, where the famous Miracle of the Mound took place. And again I found myself obtaining all my information from a clerical man.

I discovered the wisdom of that famous maxim for travellers in Italy: "If in doubt, consult the priest." This remarkable man spoke French, German, Hebrew, Latin, Greek and Italian, and immediately asked me which of these languages I would prefer. He gladly offered to show me round. And when I thanked him but said I did not want to take him from his teaching (for he was engaged when I called in giving a Greek lesson to a class of young seminarists), he replied quite cheerily: "Oh no, they can have a holiday while you are here."

It appeared that I was the first foreigner they had had for four years. The boys were delighted and ran shrilly off; and I felt rather like the Prince of Wales visiting a school, bringing with him half-holidays, tuck-shop treats and other concessions.

He then took me to a huge mound of earth outside the village, about as big as the Crystal Palace, and explained that here, in the Middle Ages, the famous miracle took place. This mound was once a *moggio* or pile of grain, owned by a rich and extremely miserly farmer. One day a beggar approached him and asked if he might have a handful of grain, as he was starving. The miser rudely refused. Whereupon the beggar—who was none other than *Nostro Signore Gesu Cristo*—raised his hand and pointed accusingly at the *moggio*, which promptly turned into a mound of earth, the beggar himself also immediately disappearing.

The priest then asked me to come back to his house. Here his aged mother made coffee for us. And I realised from the deferential way she treated him, and did not sit with us, but served us like a waitress, that he was one of those products of the Catholic Church, a peasant who wanted to learn, a Sorel.

For it is still only by entering the Church that the poor can get a good education in Italy. But then, as in the case of the Jesuit training, it is probably the best in the world. I could well understand the villagers' respect and love for this man. Not only was he clever, but also kind; I had learned earlier that, with his knowledge of German, he had interceded more than once with the *Wehrmacht*, when reprisals or some similar barbarity were being prepared.

"Yes," he said. "I spoke much German during the war." And, going over to the bookcase, he extracted the works of Goethe, pointing to a poem called *The Wanderer*.

"That poem," he said, "describes people like you."

He then insisted on reading it. In some ways it was not inappropriate; for it contains a dialogue between a foreign wanderer on Italian soil and a peasant woman, at a loss to understand why he should stop at her dwelling, which contains odd bits of stone from Greek and Roman temples, all covered with hieroglyphs, which the traveller immediately starts deciphering.

I observed that at this the likeness stopped, for my Greek was elementary.

"Ah," he said, looking at me closely, "you are then a man of modern education?"

Sadly, I had to confess I was. And he nodded his head wisely, as if to say that it takes all kinds to make a world, and I mustn't let it worry me.

I left him that morning with a feeling of inferiority, not only at his knowledge, but even more before the certainty and tranquillity of faith of this man, who had, all his life, never moved more than thirty miles from Aquila.

He who visits Italy and does not come away impregnated with the atmosphere of religion—whether he believes in or not—cannot really be said to have visited Italy. As in this village, with its miraculous mound and very Christian priest, there is not a city, town or parish in this land that does not bear some imprint of the Catholic Faith—without a corner, square or street, that has not some name glorifying the Faith. *Santa Maria Gloriosa dei Frati, Santa Maria Formosissima della Salute, Il Campo Santo dei Fedeli, La Via degli Angeli*—the names ring out from Syracuse to Domodossola. Even in the loneliest village, desolate, fossilised, forgotten, on a hill like this, a church arises with its musical title—a relic of that Age of Faith, when an immense hope inhabited these places.

CHAPTER NINE

The Land of Ovid

WE WERE NOW nearing the outward limit of
our journey, the city of Sulmona, after which
I intended turning south-west for Rome, along the
Valerian Way which has always linked the capital with
the Adriatic. Examining the map, I saw, with some
excitement, great names on the road ahead, Alba
Fucentia, Corfinium, Interpromium, Tagliacozzo—all
of them awakening my fancy with thoughts of the
Legions and those Great Companies that later roamed
the land—". . . Roman nobles," says Macaulay,
"attended by their slaves, with horses decked in scarlet,
gold and silver; fine ladies borne in litters, with silken
curtains; trumpeters, soldiers, merchants, mountebanks,
captives in chains. . . ."

Yet when I reached these places, I found them
miserable mounds of cottages and poultry-runs, desolate, unsavoury spots, with perhaps a couple of donkeys
and a goat drawn up alongside a stack of charcoal.
Alba—which was once the proud rival of Rome!
And Corfinium—which once dreamt of absorbing her!

In spite of these disillusions, the classical atmosphere
as we approached Sulmona, the birthplace of Ovid,
soon made itself felt. Our walk down the valley
took us past Roccacasale, far up on the left with
its towers and campaniles; and behind it, reaching
up still higher into the Apennines, the grey, woodless
rocks to which the village seemed to cling, becoming
one with them, part of their background, in colour as
in shape.

Ovid lived near the *Fons Amoris* of his poem. And,

as always in Italy where water springs, the valley here is suddenly green with a hundred shades of poplar, ilex and osier, recalling almost, to an Englishman, the site of Runnymede. Only southern trees upon the nearby hillside—the mulberry, fig and oleander—tell that these water-meadows are not the Scholar Gipsy's, but those of Amaryllis. Beside them the poet got out his tablets and made the notes he later used for the *Metamorphoses*. Withdrawn a little from the road, it is still possible to evoke the river-gods, hamadryads and milk-white steers of his imagination. But the main road is too near—only a quarter of a mile beyond—and down it to-day tear the lorries and buses, hooting their way in Italian style, without silencers, scaring every chicken and child within miles.

I was lucky enough to come upon a flock of sheep in the marshy ground near the river, grazing round their shepherd, who was taking them in turn and shearing them. The ones that had been cut immediately became excited, forming little groups away from their more heavily laden fellows, their heads together in discussion—like American football players. I had never seen this before, and I felt it must be peculiar to the descendants of the sheep of Virgil and Ovid (a Latin sheep still seems to me superior to the rest of its species). No doubt, however, they were behaving in a perfectly normal pecorine manner—which was even now being repeated on the banks and braes of Peebles.

Badia, where Ovid lived, is an ordinary enough little village, with its two dusty streets, nineteenth-century church and Post Office. Quite how many destructions it has undergone since the poet's day, no one seems to know. The latest was in 1799, when the French, for some inexplicable military reason, suddenly levelled it entirely. It was deserted when I arrived—one of those hot, silent noondays in Italy when one walks through the empty streets and asks oneself, "What do the people do here to pass the twenty-four hours?"

I saw an elderly man driving some oxen in a field outside and went over, hoping he might be able to direct me to the Fountain of Love. He smiled and stopped his ploughing. It must have been a question he had often heard. "There is nothing left," he said sadly. "All that tells of the Fountain of Love is the new Fountain of Victory erected on the same site."

His words were not clear to me, so I visited this place after lunch. It is, as he said, now called the Fountain of Victory, and commemorates one of Victor Emmanuel's many skirmishes in the recent heroic period. The old fountain has been completely transformed and is now surmounted by something in the style, if not in the dimensions, of Trafalgar Square.

I was more interested in a small crucifix nearby, in which Christian and pagan sentiment had been unconsciously wedded. For some irreligious peasant had used it, this symbol of our Faith, to support a vine-shoot—so that it was a sort of ghastly symbol, of life embracing death, the delicate, green tendrils entwining the legs of the Saviour. And yet—this is no more than the directions of Virgil, now a Father of the Church! In the *Georgics* he recommends that the vine shall be draped about whatever upright happens to be handy—a viticultural habit which is common enough in Southern Italy. Nature is so lavish here, I have often noted, that the vines are left to their own devices, growing almost wild, their only support willows or poplars or, as here on the site of the *Fons Amoris*, whatever upright they find.

I walked down an avenue of a double row of maple trees that patterned the ground with wind-blown shadows, until I came at the end to the convent of Badia Morronese, in whose cloister I caught a glimpse of strolling monks. Here too were vines, on trellises and pergolas—the muscat with its purple, dusty grape; the sweet *pizzutello*, elongated like some tiny gherkin, sometimes black, sometimes silver. Around the pillars in the cloister clustered myrtle and rose bushes, and in the centre stood a large almond, already heavy with fruit—the tree which the ancients said was placed on the grave of Narcissus, as a symbol of the lover.

These surroundings have indeed something of the half-lines, the sad hemistiches of the lyric poets of Rome —"grass softer than sleep", "caves with the gadding vine o'ergrown"; truly this land of Ovid is where "a golden race of peacocks dyed in laughing beauty trod".

The village of Badia has other memories, however, than those of the Latin poets—in the eyes of the local inhabitants, of far greater importance. For it is also the land of Peter the Hermit.

One should never forget in Italy that the Roman Empire is still looked upon, even by many educated people, as having been specially created by God so that, at the right moment, Christianity could step in and take it over, reform it and replace it. Horace, Virgil, Ovid, even Augustus—all these men existed to prepare the soil for the Church. As pagan artists or administrators they are much less. Indeed, Dante, the typical Italian, has put them all in Limbo; even the "good Augustus" and the great Virgil are benighted for this reason, for having been born before Christ:

> *vissi a Roma sotto il buon Augusto*
> *ai tempi dei Dei falsi e bugiardi. . . .*[1]

This explains, perhaps in part, why Peter the Hermit is a greater local figure than Ovid. He lived in a cave here, where he was persuaded in 1294, against his better judgment, to go to Rome and become Pope Celestino V. It was hoped that a man of such piety

[1] I lived in Rome under the good Augustus, in the days of the false and lying gods.

would reform the Papacy fallen, as it did from time to time, into evil ways. Like Mahomet, he left his cave for greater things. Unlike Mahomet, however, he lasted only five months, and then, unable to put up with the secular turmoil of Papal politics—the Orsinis, the Colonnas and their domestic squabbles—he renounced the tiara and retired to the cave again. You can still see it on the burnt mountainside above Badia— now the site of an elaborate convent bearing his name.

Dante, who loathed an *indifferente* almost more than anyone else, put Peter the Hermit in Limbo, together with the Latin poets and other unbaptised persons, *per aver fatto il gran rifiuto*, for "not having tried". He considered that such a good man, by shirking his responsibility and the opportunity he had of reforming the Papacy, was no longer a good man. However that may be, Peter is said to be the most Abruzzese of the saints; and without appreciating his superb gesture, "the only Pope who has ever given up the tiara after wearing it, a spiritual Charles V", one cannot understand his fellow-countrymen.

A number of his followers founded his Order after "the great refusal"—"*i poveri eremiti di Celestino*," practising the same form of asceticism in a cave. They wore hair-shirts, scooped out little niches in the walls and put skulls in them, enjoined reverence for the sanctuary, devotion in religious exercises and general discretion of life. But their influence was, for some reason, considered unhealthy by the later Popes, and they were suppressed. Their founder, too, spent his last days, not in his cave, as he would have wished, but in prison—where his successor in the chair of St. Peter, the dynamic and irascible Boniface VIII, sent him, lest he might suddenly change his mind and want to be Pope again.

I am always glad whenever I think of this incident, to remember that if Dante put Peter the Hermit in

Limbo for not showing enough spirit, he put his successor, the efficient Boniface, seven rungs lower, almost at the bottom of the Inferno, for showing too much.

That religion is the chief, one might almost say the only, intellectual pursuit of these people is clear from this love of the anchorite, as well as from the absolute inferiority of civil architecture to clerical in the Abruzzi. In the most miserable little village on a mound, where pigs, goats and chickens share the exterior—sometimes even the interior—life of the inhabitants, a church of considerable proportions will arise, containing its quota of priests, seminarists and self-constituted guides. This is perhaps why the history books claim that the Abruzzi is the most Christian region of Italy. The gospel took some time to penetrate here, as one would expect. Paganism was a hardy plant and the Virgin had yet to replace Demeter. In a village like Bazzano, just outside Aquila, poor St. Clara was burnt alive in an "ardent oven" (*forno ardente*) for her faith. The Lombards, too, who lorded it here for the next 300 years, also retarded the propagation of the Faith, in their usual violent way. But Christianity slowly wormed its way in, and, once installed, assumed its most extreme form in the Abruzzi—the anchorite. To be completely Christian has here signified from early times to flee the world, to be a hermit. Peter is the classic case.

But surely the oddest reason for becoming a hermit must be that of the Frenchman, Stéphane Gautier, who arrived here in 1838, and announced his intention of living in an anfractuosity of the Mount Avicenna. He said that a celestial vision had instructed him. He accordingly installed himself; and the local inhabitants, as was their custom with hermits, brought him food and drink. He prayed and had a chalice and kept a tame starling. To avoid the evil eye, he carried a

F

bunch of badger's hair and the tooth of a wolf that had been killed in the spring. He was seen hanging his cowl on a sunbeam and it was rumoured that, shortly, when he had prayed enough, he would run through Italy writing on the gates of every city the name of the Virgin; and that the Pope would make him a *cavaliere di Cristo*.

And then one day the police appeared and took him away—to the consternation of the local inhabitants. A few days later it was learned that he had been handed over to the French justice—for having taken part in an attempt on the life of Louis Philippe, just over two years before.

CHAPTER TEN

The Germans Again

SULMONA, WHERE I intended spending several days, is at the end of this valley, in the richest, most fertile part of the Abruzzi. It seems a fairly well-to-do town, a sort of Maidstone, whose staple industry is sugar-plums. Only by a considerable effort of the imagination can one feel, with the guide-book, that it "still has much of the shrine it once was to the worship of Vesta and Apollo". On the contrary, it was the first city I visited on my donkey-ride which might, by any stretch of the imagination, be described as *mondaine*. It had three cinema palaces; a hotel which for some reason, still bore the royal arms of Savoyard Italy; and a cavalry barracks. Indeed, one of the most notable things about Sulmona was the number of soldiers in battle-dress I saw lolling about. Their presence had one great advantage for us, however. Being the Italian Army, their cavalry was cavalry —not a lot of tin trucks, as in the cavalry of the more advanced nations; they were horsed, or rather muled. And Masceri quickly made for the commissariat department where, he maintained, he could obtain a quantity of fodder very cheaply, perhaps gratuitously, through a friend of his in the quartermaster's department. For we were now approaching his *patria*; he was born in nearby Anversa.

The first result of this was that I was introduced to a number of his friends, including a nephew who was doing his military service at the barracks, but who, like so many Italian soldiers, supplemented his pay by commercial activity.

This man owned a small itinerant bric-a-brac stall, which he used to station in off-duty hours outside the café where I spent the *siesta*, reading the newspapers. He had chosen this spot well, for it was the centre of a most variegated life; the scene not only of other street-sellers but also of loafers of all kinds, including those urchins, without whom no Italian scene is complete, little Beppos, whose life seems to be spent basking in the beams of the sun, eating boiled beans and playing *mora*.[1]

This nephew of Masceri's, who sold among other things fountain-pens and pencils on a tray, was irresistible to watch. I could never keep my eyes off him; for to watch him selling a propelling pencil was to watch a work of art. From the expressions of almost religious ecstasy on his face as he propelled it before a prospective customer, one half expected to come out of the end, not a lead, but the Holy Ghost. He also owned a large Alsatian dog, said to have been left behind by the Gestapo on their hasty departure in 1944. This dog used to bark beside his stall for no apparent reason, and in such an excruciating manner, that one evening, almost before I knew what I was doing, I had run over and asked him to silence it; for I am allergic to the bark of dogs. For answer, most affably, he offered me a fountain-pen with one hand, and a large stick with the other, implying that I should beat it.

"But I don't want to beat it," I said.

"Go on!" he said. "It's a German dog!"

I took the stick and menaced it. The animal stopped barking and looked at me sideways. I hit it lightly on

---

[1] *Mora* is an admirably Italian pastime, requiring speed but not depth of mind, and as it is played with the fingers, no props. You throw out one, two, three or four fingers as you wish at your adversary, announcing the number at the same time. If he does not throw out the same number simultaneously, he loses. But if he does—and announces it—he wins, and takes over the lead. It is played with a violent, mounting interest and frequently leads to blows.

the back, and it began to whimper a little. But I could not bring myself to strike it really hard. Whereupon, the fountain-pen seller suddenly seized the stick and began belabouring it soundly. To my immense surprise, when he stopped, the animal began to wag its tail, making little sounds of pleasure; and then frisked about at our feet with its tail between its legs, like a flirting puppy, completely silenced.

"It's a German," he explained; "but he's not a bad dog. He has a heart."

This, I thought, was typical of the attitude of the Italians towards the Germans, in spite of the belabouring *they* are always receiving at the hands of these robust northerners. The Italians have such a long tradition, I suppose, of Germanic invasion and oppression since Brennus first said *Vae Victis*, that they are indifferent to all the suffering these hearty folk have been inflicting on them regularly every few decades, for the last two millennia. They seem to look on them without hate, love or pleasure—but simply as they do the *scirocco*, a seasonable, unaccountable work of God, that may have been sent for some good purpose, to be revealed hereafter. A man in my hotel in Sulmona told me, almost hilariously, that the *first* German to make a *really* bad impression in the peninsula was Albion the Lombard, who beheaded an Italian nobleman in A.D. 613, married his daughter, and then made her drink wine out of her father's skull, which he had made into a drinking cup. This, he seemed to think, was quite in keeping with their recent behaviour—even justified it.

Another Italian, a trifle more critical of the Teutons, once told me that what he disliked about them more than anything else was their language, which he considered barbaric. "A language," he said, "where you have to wait until the end of five yards for a verb. Who can tell what they want while it's going on?"

And he told me of a German captain who was giving instructions to his lieutenant from a train window in a station, while waiting to leave in 1944. ". . . And that Lieutenant," he said, "never knew whether he was to come up, or go down, or come here, or go there, or get on or get off—because the train left before the captain had got to the *von* or *zu* or *um* or whatever it was at the end! There's a language for you! Is English like that?"

The last instance of German vandalism which I heard of in these parts concerned a white marble angel over a rich man's tomb. The Germans had defaced this in a most remarkable way. . . .

They had had shot sixteen young men of this village out of hand in 1943, and I asked the local priest to tell me why. For answer, he led me to this angel in the cemetery. "One of the first acts of the Germans," he said, "when they made our village into a headquarters, was to camouflage our cemetery. We stand, as you see, on a hill, and are a good landmark for aeroplanes. We can be seen"—he pointed around proudly—"from as far away as Sulmona."

He then described how the Germans carried out this camouflage.

"They did it," he said, "with nets and paint and foliage. This churchyard became a jungle. Wherever you went, you tripped over cords and imitation trees, and bits of cloth painted to look like rock. Two families who lived in a cottage over there were evicted, because it was considered *uncamouflageable*. And their property was blown up. A large canvas screen"—he pointed to the church—"was erected round one corner of the west chancel. But the most difficult problem of all was this cemetery. It is, as you see, surrounded by these fine white walls. And there were several big marble angels, like this one, over the graves. The German colonel said the walls and the statues were to be dazzle-painted. And if this failed, the statues were to be removed entirely! But first, they would wait to get an official report from the *Luftwaffe*. They were anxious, you will understand, at this time, not to antagonise public opinion too much." It was 1943.

"But that *Luftwaffe* report was unfavourable! From as far away as Sulmona, the pilots said, our cemetery could be seen. And so a squad of soldiers removed all the statues. All, at least, except this one." He pointed to the sorry-looking angel which towered above us, from which the dazzle streaks of green and brown had not yet been entirely removed.

His eyes narrowed and a violent look transformed his features. "But while they were doing it," he said, "a member of one of the families whose tombs were being desecrated, a Partisan, *shot* one of the German soldiers. In a fit of righteous indignation. And then"— he looked at me meaningly—"you know the result. . . ."

Someone I hope, will one day write a book entitled, *Anecdotic History of the Hun in Italy, Twentieth Century*. It will not deal with the usual things— resistance, atrocities, parachuting and so forth; it will be about those little day-to-day Teutonisms which every Italian in his heart despises—despises rather than hates; the things the Hun did unnecessarily: absconding with statues, cutting pictures out of frames, interfering with old people's hobbies, such as looking through telescopes at stars on clear nights, abducting domestic animals; military actions for which only the French really have a term, *les petites conneries boches*.

CHAPTER ELEVEN

An English Idyll

AS A RESULT of Masceri's connections in Sulmona, we obtained certain advantages, of which free fodder was but one. The most agreeable of all was now to come. I had by now taken a number of photographs of our Sabine journey which I wished to develop and enlarge; and Masceri said he knew a photographer who, he thought, would allow me to use his dark-room. We accordingly visited this man, whom we found standing in the middle of his shop, evidently on the point of going out. He was dressed in a grey wool sweater and black trousers. On his head was a tin hat, and in his hand a revolver. (Is everyone in this city, I asked myself, a soldier?)

"I am," he explained, "a member of the newly constituted militia for maintaining order. It is not unlike your English Home Guard. I am a sergeant and have taken part, in both wars, in altogether sixteen major actions. I started as a private at Vittorio Veneto. And finished, as you see, with this rank, at the rear-guard action of Slinkerish."

Wishing to humour this bellicose photographer, on account of the dark-room, I said I imagined that Slinkerish was one of those actions in the desert.

"In Albania," he corrected.

I did not ask which side he had been fighting for, as I had learnt by now how tactless this question can be in Italy. But he saw that I was English, and it was soon clear where his sympathies lay. He became immensely friendly. He insisted on showing me all his equipment in the cellar (which I had hoped might be a dark-room). It contained revolvers, rifles, sub-machine guns, grenades and other weapons, all of which British aviators had showered on him at various intervals during the war for his Partisan activities—and which he had illegally retained. His cellar formed a veritable arsenal—but which, I thankfully observed, was for putting down rather than fomenting disorder.

"If I had a platoon under my charge now, things would be different with these Communists," he said darkly. "What is it you want? To enlarge? By all means. Come up and meet my wife. She likes Englishmen."

Not quite seeing the connection, I allowed him, however, to lead me upstairs. He added on the way that his wife's partiality for young Englishmen had started during the war, in Albania, where she had harboured a batch of escaped airmen.

In a neat little sitting-room, I was surprised to find a young lady, at least twenty years younger than he, of great beauty, with a blooming complexion and extremely vivacious—an Albanian he had met during the war! She had, he explained, only recently joined him in Italy and could speak no Italian; so he acted as interpreter. A necklace of very fine silver chain was wound at least eight times around her throat, which was whiter than alabaster; it then hung down in loops, covering her breast most charmingly. A closely-fitting jacket set off her figure with wanton elegance; and rose-coloured shoes displayed to my admiring eye the dainty shape of a tiny foot. She put out her hand to me in a languishing manner; and I dealt with it urbanely, in the Continental style.

Her husband suggested that I should eat and drink, excusing himself at the same time, as he was bound for his "home guard" activities, and must leave us. In this way, the Albanian lady and I found ourselves suddenly alone—somewhat to my surprise, I must confess. She asked me what I would like. It was half-past four, so I made signs to my mouth with my hand that to this Englishman a cup of tea would be most acceptable. But these signs she only appeared to take for—amorous indications! I attempted therefore to make the action of drinking from a cup—whereupon she ran to the shelf and took down a dictionary of English and Serbian, in which she picked out the words "I—LOVE—ENGLISHMEN".

The word *love* in English has a fairly general meaning, it is true; but I felt that the time had now come to make a move, particularly when I considered what manner of man her husband was. But she only smiled adorably and ran out of the room, returning almost immediately with a plate of delicious iced cakes and a bottle of *Strega*. I could hardly refuse such hospitality. And for the next three-quarters of an hour we sat talking by signs, eating, and frequently referring to the dictionary, with which we said things that might, I fear, have ended rather seriously had not her husband's sudden return put an end to this *marivaudage*.

He, however, appeared delighted to see me still there, shook my hand warmly—and winked at his wife! To which she gave a little pout of disapproval. It was only then that I realised that I had not behaved correctly. But they remained charming and hospitable throughout the rest of the tea, which was later supplemented by the photographer's brandy. They entreated me not only to use the dark-room whenever I liked, but said that, if I were staying a few more days, they would put a bedroom at my disposal. The advantages of this were so considerable that I accepted.

The Albanian lady was, I found, of a particularly amorous disposition. Of her character, I fear I can say little. For a person with whom no verbal communication is possible defies a description based on words. They gave me a pleasant room, decorated with all manner of chintzes and elegant walnut furniture and silk hangings. It was next to the dark-room, and here I worked with the enlarger. She often came into my bedroom, whenever I rang the bell for nourishment, which was fairly often, generally when I was tired of classifying my prints. She sometimes brought iced cakes, sometimes a cup of coffee, or sometimes nothing but her lovely face, always gay, always smiling. At first I allowed these visits to be very frequent, but after three days, in which I had done hardly any work at all, I had to curtail them, so as not to lose too much time in the tenderness of love—of which, I must say, that pretty Albanian was complete mistress.

This little diversion, the only one of its kind during my donkey-ride, showed me in the most charming way imaginable the affection with which my race is still regarded by certain foreigners. After all the sad things I had heard about our decay and eclipse, I do not exaggerate when I say that this incident reanimated me. In this land, always subject to foreigners, so many Italians had told me that the English influence of the eighteenth and nineteenth century is dying, has indeed already been replaced by others, more vital and progressive. And I had had ample opportunity, even in Sulmona, to confirm this sad state of affairs.

Outside my own hotel was a sign in a freshly painted shop window, TO BAGDAD AND BACK IN FOUR DAYS! TRAVEL T.W.A.! An enterprising American air line had recently opened up its office! Before this window all day long circulated a little group of loafers, young and old, admiring models of gleaming silver aeroplanes and beautiful stewardesses, chromo-photographs of distant capitals and black men in feathered head-dresses. . . . But, alas, by the very nature of their idleness unable to afford the trip.

And then, in the Sulmona cinemas, everything spoke of far-away America. Opposite the big statue of Ovid, the Cinema Ovidio was showing, I think, *Angels in Boots*, with Jennifer Jones and Gregory Peck—magnetic names which have more influence in Italy to-day than all the counsellors, clerks and consuls of Her Britannic Majesty.

To generalise, one may say then that the British influence has how been replaced in the Peninsula; but by *two* others, both in the great classical tradition of foreign interference—the American and the Russian. No doubt they will, like those of the Goth, Hun, Saracen, Lombard, Spaniard, French, German and the rest of them throughout the centuries, later be replaced by others—as cynical Italians will tell you—by the Indian, African, Cuban, Chinese. Why not? But at the moment these two are flourishing. They are supposed to be in deadly conflict, but they seem to me much less dissimilar, in Italy, than they think.

The Russian, as everyone knows, wishes to abolish property, murder the parliamentarians, overthrow the Army, Navy and police force and establish its own; to introduce a new ruling class selected by itself—and be *efficient*—in short, to replace the top by the bottom. The other, the American movement, wishes to bring everything up-to-date overnight; to make hundreds of thousands of *lire* by "time is money", to live in cocktail bars, sell Coca-cola on the Grand Canal and rush about in gleaming motor-cars—being equally *efficient*.

Quite apart from them, quite distinct I consider, is the old Italy, flea-ridden, patriarchal, wine-drinking, *in*efficient—the *troisième force* of the Peninsula; but which is so unsuited to modern conditions that it is having to compromise with the two powerful adversaries on its soil. This delicate process of adjustment is now going on.

An interesting example of this America-Russia match—on the Italian pitch—was to be found in a nearby village which was in an uproar on the

subject of a plaque to be affixed to the war memorial
—to commemorate those who died fighting for Americans, Germans, English and Communists during the
recent wars. This memorial was unusual in that it
commemorated three different wars. The village, too
poor even to erect one for the 1918 upheaval, was
using the Victor Emmanuel equestrian monument of
1861 for all three convulsions.

In a café in the main square, the local schoolmaster
explained to me why this memorial is dividing family
from family, brother from brother, generation from
generation in Italy to-day.

"My brother," he said, "was killed in Africa in 1942
fighting for the Germans against the Americans. He
was decorated three times and did his duty. My
nephew was killed in Bologna in 1944, fighting for
the Americans against the Germans. He also did
his duty. My wife's brother became a Partisan. He
was a Communist and was killed after the war fighting the Neo-Fascists. Did he do his duty? I think
we may say that, according to his lights, he did. Now,
how is the memory of all these men to be recorded
on that single monument?" He pointed to the Victor
Emmanuel statue.

"By separate plaques," I suggested.

"But surely a war memorial is something which
commemorates those who have died for a common
cause, is it not? Can these men be said to have done
that?"

"They all died, in one way or another, for Italy," I said.

"Exactly! That is my point of view. Be hanged
which side you were on, so long as you died with a
rifle in your hand and *Italia!* on your lips. But that,
I fear, is not the view of the civic authorities to-day.
The Mayor is a Communist. And so is most of his
Council. They contend that only my Partisan brother-
in-law is a true patriot. Only he may be commemorated

on the plaque. On the other hand, a year ago, we had a *demo-cristiano* Mayor. And he drew up a list of all those, like my nephew, who died fighting for the *Americans!*"

"And how about the one who was killed fighting in Libya for the Germans?" I asked.

"He is not mentioned at all. By either side. Although he was the most wounded, the most decorated and, in my opinion, the bravest of all. If a bit of an ass."

"And all these should, you think," I said, pointing to the monument again, "be associated there with Victor Emmanuel?"

"Yes. But there isn't room for them all on that statue."

"Well, why not put some of them on the Dante memorial?" I said. For I have often noted in Italy the habit of coupling on every possible occasion the names of Dante and Victor Emmanuel as the two great, representative Italian patriots. (As ill-assorted pair as you could imagine really—the well-fed Savoyard and the ascetic Tuscan.)

"No," said the schoolmaster very firmly. And he refused to talk to me any more after such a sacrilegious suggestion. . . .

Inscriptions on monuments in Italian villages are often indicative in a most interesting way like this of the constantly changing political scene, so mercurial in the eyes of the phlegmatic British democrat. In another village I read about this inscription on a fountain:

> *A Pio Sovrano,*
> *Al sommo Pastore,*
> *Noi miseri figli*
> *Offriamo l'amore.*[1]

The date was 1857.

[1] To the sovereign Pontiff, to the great Pastor we, his unworthy children, offer our love.

In the same village, in the church, the following contradictory inscription on another plaque was to be found—written only three years later, after the defeat of the above-mentioned Pontiff by the Savoyards:

Vittorio Emmanuele II, il Duce valoroso
di Magenta qui, venendo dal Piemonte,
colse su questa monte, i primi omaggi
del popolo di nostro paese.[1]

At a distance, then, of just over three years these *miseri figli*, after having offered their hearts to Pope Pius XI, offered them to his mortal enemy, Victor Emmanuel II!

But this is no speciality of the Italians. In other countries, people offer their hearts with a good deal of facility to new pastors—provided they are successful.

[1] Victor Emmanuel II, the valiant General of Magenta, here, descending from Piedmont, received the first homage of the people, from our village.

CHAPTER TWELVE

Masceri's Relations

THE DISTANCE BETWEEN Sulmona and Anversa degli Abruzzi, the birthplace of Masceri, cannot be much more than thirty miles, but the land we crossed was so difficult that the journey took nearly three days. Almost immediately after leaving Sulmona the road mounts, and soon the fertile, featureless plains and rounded hillsides of the valley of the Gizio were replaced by deep gorges and fast-flowing rivers—a land where neither industry nor commerce exist, only olives and vines and occasionally a fruit tree in the rocks. Nor does one see any more of those solitary towers of the Middle Ages which populate the lower valleys. The shriek of the vulture circling above, the bray of the donkey, the dull thunder of the Sagittario River 200 feet below—these sounds are enough to make one understand why D'Annunzio chose this setting for his most gloomy plays, a land dedicated entirely, one would say, to those wild Eumenides he introduces so often, to comment on the scenes of violence and passion of his native Abruzzi.

The mountains ahead seemed for the most part clothed in patchwork forests, even to the summits, through which an occasional flinty peak would present itself, rising up into the clouds. Where there were no trees, it was one of the most dreary regions imaginable, a land of rocks and stones, entirely devoid of grass. Unfortunately, not long after our departure rain set in.

I put on a mackintosh and Masceri extracted an old Army gas-cape from beneath the hay on Pepe's back. Under the moisture, the ears of our donkey, normally spruce and upstanding, became limp and flaccid,

scarcely raising themselves at the fierce, barbaric cries
of the muleteer. I think that long companionship with
animals had made these sounds almost second nature
to Masceri. For they appeared not to make the slightest
difference to the donkey, which continued at the same
unvarying gait, over hill and dale, through bog and
briar, in the light and in the dark, regardless of
whether anyone were on its back or not.

We tramped and stumbled on in the gathering gloom,
up a track which Masceri professed to know, an advance
that was so slow that towards nine o'clock on the
third night, I was for dossing down in a barn and
eating our remaining provisions. But Masceri was sure
that his relations would be delighted to receive us,
even if we arrived after midnight.

"This is the valley of Molino, the murderer," he
said, encouragingly. "The *carabinieri* couldn't catch
him. He used to lay in wait for travellers at night.
And whoever they were, Italian or foreign, they all
finished in the same way. From a tree."

"They caught him finally, I hope," I said.

"Yes, finally. But it was a loss to the countryside.
He used to take from the rich and give to the poor."

"Did you count among the poor?"

"No. If you mean by that, did I benefit? But he was
a fine fellow, all the same. There are few of his kind
about to-day."

"How about Giuliano, in Sicily?" I said.

"Ah, but Sicily . . ." He shrugged his shoulders.

As we walked on, I reflected that the old Italy of
not so long ago, the Italy of the bandits and the black-
eyed beauties, had indeed gone—when robberies, mur-
ders and all kinds of atrocities were being daily committed around the traveller. In the few inhabited
places we passed, not so much as a dog barked. A
universal silence had set in, and except for the sound
of the hooves, the occasional croaking of frogs from

G

some distant pool or morass, and the hoarse ejaculations of Masceri, we might have been on the moon itself.

I have said elsewhere that our donkey remained indifferent to everything we did to him. There was one exception, however. We could present him with almost any upward slope, but he disliked going down-hill. It was at a downhill passage—one of the few we came upon—that I was now taken unawares on his back. This animal which, for over six weeks, had given no sign of mental, even physical life, apart from the forward movement of his legs (which seemed mechanical rather than anatomical), suddenly galvanised into a trot, or rather into something which was a cross between a trot and a canter, extraordinarily uncomfortable and not unlike riding in a tank. Masceri had dropped behind and, although he now ran after me yelling instructions, he could not catch up. I had moreover, dropped the rope which served as a rein.

"Pull his left ear!" yelled Masceri. I once took some pride in myself as a horseman and would never have stooped to such an action, but now I found myself, as we gathered speed, lunging forward desperately, grasping for the ear, as if it were a brake. But the animal's head was down and it was out of reach. Pepe now began to make extraordinary noises, as if some terrible carnal excitement possessed him; and then began to gallop, a most unpleasing gait for a donkey. I held on by my grip, which returned to me miraculously, and by the animal's ample mane. Odd stones and flints flew up beneath his hoofs and struck me forcibly in the face. My position by now, however diverting for the reader, was most disagreeable to me—on the back of a maddened animal, dashing down towards a steep gorge, my guide and protector far behind.

No doubt we would have had quite an escapade had not another donkey suddenly appeared at a turning behind a gate and began to "hee-haw" amorously.

Whereupon Pepe stopped—as abruptly as he had started—and was within a second nuzzling the other, who appeared as delighted as he did at the meeting! I detached myself breathlessly from his neck, and Masceri ran up puffing.

"A lady donkey!" he explained.

Gathering the rope, he forcibly separated Pepe from his new friend. Their desperate "hee-haws" as they were parted sounded inexpressively melancholy to me—and I bore them no grudge.

Towards eleven o'clock the rain stopped, and I calculated that once we had crossed the mountain ahead we would see the village above us. This was so. Anversa degli Abruzzi lies at the entrance to a gorge, an ancient place girt with walls and turrets, perched high on an abyss above the dark waters of the Sagittario.

An hour later we were walking through its deserted streets, welcomed by a horrid squalling of cats. Whether due to my state of mind, or to the real condition of the village, I do not know, but Anversa degli Abruzzi, reputed to be one of the most sinister places in Italy—the scene of D'Annunzio's tragedy, *La Fiaccola sotto il Moggio*—seemed to me most agreeable.

Although it was past midnight, Masceri's relations came down and kindly offered to put us up. A blousy woman with grey hair seemed to be a cousin. She said she was sorry, they had no spare room in the house; would we mind sleeping in the barn? I naturally accepted, and she escorted us behind the house, pointing on the way to a heap of straw in the yard. For curiosity's sake, I asked if there was such a thing as a bed, but this appeared to exist only in the house; and she pointed again to the straw. For more reasons than one, I avoided this straw, with which Masceri plentifully bestrewed himself. I lay instead at the other end of the barn, covered by a mackintosh.

But I slept fitfully. At times, I seemed plunged

in the deepest, most comforting slumbers; at others, I awoke sweating, my head teeming with shapeless dreams. I concluded I must have caught a chill during our depressing ride, and towards three in the morning rose to look for my kit-bag and an aspirin. But I could not find the key to its padlock. Moreover, Masceri had removed the bag from the donkey's back and was now using it as a pillow.

I went over to see if there was any way of withdrawing it without waking him. But the man was sleeping the profoundest sleep I have ever seen, as death itself. I spoke; I shouted. Not a movement did he make. His ugly face reminded me of one of those uncouth sarcophagi of paladins you see in French churches. So strong and rigid was it that I became almost frightened and thought he was really dead. And I had to bend down and bellow within a few inches of his ear before he awoke.

"Masceri!" I yelled. "Wake up! You must search Pepe and see if the key has fallen in the straw."

For about three seconds his eyes opened and he glared at me with a wild surmise. Then, with a start, like some animal let off the leash, he leapt to his feet, uttered a blood-curdling cry and bounded to the door. He wrenched it open and disappeared into the night in spite of my cries, in the direction of the stable. This conduct, together with other odd remarks on the journey, convinced me that I was in the company of a man of a not entirely balanced mind. However, I was too tired to worry about him so, failing to find the key, I could only return to the rug, where I fell into a doze, which continued fitfully for the rest of the night. . . .

I awoke the next morning to find him already at the door with Pepe, whose hoof he was examining. I decided not to say anything, but to wait for him to refer to his curious behaviour. He appeared however, most preoccupied and taciturn.

"Last night, *signorino*," he said at length, without looking up, "I had a dream. That you came up to me and said 'Get up, Masceri. And see if Pepe's shoe has fallen in the straw!' It sounds impossible, but I must have walked to the stable in my sleep. For this morning I found myself in the straw beside Pepe. And look!" He lifted the hoof of the donkey and pointed to a loose shoe beneath. "That is what I found in the straw. It is surely a bad omen for the journey."

I was tired of Masceri and his omens!

"I told you *I* had lost something," I said irritably. "Something far more important than a shoe, which can be replaced at any time. The key to my kitbag! Short of cutting it open, we have no money now."

This kitbag was of leather, the finest money could buy in Oxford Street, and I did not wish to mutilate it. I suddenly became very Anglo-Saxon. While we were examining the heavy padlock, Masceri's cousin, our hostess, came in. She also examined it gravely, and then said: "A foreign lock. After lunch we will get Grandad to open it."

"What does he know of locks?" I said sceptically.

"He has been in America," she said.

There seemed nothing else to do but to wait the morning and follow her advice. True to my principles, therefore, I set out for the church after breakfast, hoping to find the priest and discover something about Anversa from him while we waited for Grandad.

Wherever I passed pigs rooted and poultry fluttered, goats bleated and kids scampered. Most of the population crowded to the doors and balconies to stare. Five small boys accompanied me on my way. The only sensible creatures, I thought, were the donkeys; they regarded me stolidly and went on eating. Already I began to feel something sinister about this town and its staring population, in keeping with what I had read of in D'Annunzio. And I was alone in the

church, examining a dilapidated font, when it occurred
to me that I was myself the object of examination.
A pair of eyes were staring at me through a hole in the
door. Annoyed at being continually observed (and now
even in the church!), I rushed out and scared away the
urchin whom the eyes belonged to. He ran squealing
off, putting out his tongue.

There was little of interest in the church, and I
soon found myself looking for the priest. He was
not to be found—the reason for which became apparent.
In the back of the north chancel, alone in the church,
sat a group of about a dozen little girls, with handker-
chiefs over their heads, giggling under the benevolent
eye of a small, rotund monk who was taking them in
turn to a closet-like box at the wall, where they were
each presumably confessing to the priest, a corner of
whose soutane I could see sticking out behind the
curtain. Each stayed about a minute and came out as
she had gone in, giggling. It would be interesting to
know to what sins these five-year-olds confessed—apart
from coveting Maria's sweets. I did not wait until this
performance was finished, for I found something even
more interesting in the other transept.

I found a quantity of ants. They were dragging a
fragment of wood they had discovered across the
paving-stones to a pillar where a long train of them
disappeared, presumably into some honeycomb beneath,
where they were building a city.

I have heard of ants undermining buildings before.
And these were the largest I have ever seen, like small
termites. My inclination on seeing an ant-heap is
always to put my foot on it; I do not like these
Socialistic little creatures. But on this occasion I took
the bit of wood they were dragging away, and
replaced it by a fragment of dog-dung I found at the
door, of similar shape, size and colour. And the desire
of these insects for something to do was perfectly

satisfied. They all banded together again and began tugging again.

Before such feverish concerted activity it is impossible not to feel a certain admiration—even a certain fellow-feeling. For are we not all in a sense ants? If in the civilisations to come you imprison me in Siberia, I shall start *doing* something: learning the language, making raffia baskets, armaments, digging ditches—being busy. Just as if I were forced to work in a factory in Pittsburgh I should, I suppose, start turning out armatures and dynamos and meters, automatically, pointlessly.

At midday I returned to lunch with our hosts, a meal conducted in a patriarchal style, the three men being seated, while women came and went around us, fetching and carrying bowls, flasks and plates throughout. After luncheon the "lock-opener" (Grandad, as they called him), was brought before me. He was a little old man of at least seventy, with long, white hair, and he was led by a small boy, for he was quite blind. He carried a stick with which he tapped things. He was seated before me and I was aware of two eyes, sparkling with the brightness of a ferret's, which were turned upon me. Only the fact that they did not blink told me that they saw nothing.

"Give me the lock!" his voice quavered.

My kitbag was placed on a chair before him, and a pair of skinny hands began to stray over it, finally fastening on the padlock. One of them then transferred itself to a pocket of his coat, from which it extracted a skewer-like object and, with a skill which was truly remarkable, after three or four manipulations within the lock—it sprang open!

I was at once delighted—and appalled. This lock, I had been assured in London, would guard my possessions if I travelled through Arabia itself. I thanked him; and then ventured to put a question—for he had been described as a "lock-opener", and I wondered if this were a regular profession in these parts.

"On what work", I asked, "do you normally find yourself employed?"

"What's he say?" said the old man, who appeared to be as deaf as he was blind, turning his head.

"What is your normal work?" I shouted. "On what sort of problems are you normally engaged, IN YOUR PROFESSION?"

"Everything," said the old man complacently. "Everything. I have opened every sort of lock and door in my time. And never a complaint. My clients have always been satisfied. And have frequently contributed to my expenses. Come, boy, we must go!"

"May I have my bag?" I shouted.

Without a word, he held it out and I extracted 300 *lire*, which I placed in the harmless-looking, gnarled fingers of his outstretched right hand.

One of the women now appeared with a flask of wine. She poured him out a large glassful, which, without a word, he engulfed; and the boy led him away.

"Is he not staying?" I asked, pointing to the luncheon still on the table.

"He has more work. He will return," I was told.

That evening I slept in the hotel, as I had little wish to repeat my experience of the previous night in the barn with Masceri. But the atmosphere of D'Annunzio was to be felt even here.

I was given a room in which his terrible tragedy might have taken place. Large and scantily furnished, it contained one of those tester-beds which writers of historical novels are so fond of introducing into their works. Over the heavy, monumental chimney-piece hung a pictorial representation of Petrarch's *Trionfo della Morte*, in which the artist displayed an interest in human physical decomposition bordering almost on indecency. Death was represented by a black-clad horseman riding over three tombs. In the first of these lay a young girl of great beauty, apparently freshly dead. In the next was her body after some days, perhaps weeks, exhaling a disagreeable odour; and in the third her skeleton. An old priest stood beside these tombs, apparently explaining these different phases of extinction to three beautiful young men, all elegantly dressed, with falcons in their gloved hands, who were listening gravely to his cautionary tale.

D'Annunzio's tragedy about this town is in the same vein—about death. *La Fiaccola sotto il Moggio* tells of an ancient Anversa family in decay, of peasant sexual fury, and of the sinister *serparo* with his sack of snakes. It is distinguished by a sort of sad sensuality in which the bestial side of man is uppermost, together with his most extreme physical sensations, of sight, sound, touch and smell. As in the novels of Thomas Hardy, Nature also becomes a character—the Abruzzi's wildest gorges, with her terrestrial, aerial, even solar manifestations—more important than the human beings, and their petty rites, religions and superstitions. Nature creates these people, he seems to say, for no particular reason; and for no particular reason she destroys them.

> . . . silently
> she was buried—silently;
> and every face around her
> was as the sepulchral stone,
> as the stone that is placed above
> the dark and secret thing. . . .

D'Annunzio is that typically modern man—the æsthete-airman—normally a product of more virile northern climes than the Abruzzi. To read about his life to-day is like retiring across five centuries to the period of the great *condottieri*.

Before the First World War he was regarded merely as a sensuous decadent, whose claim to distinction was his exquisite sense of beauty and his mastery of language (*Député de la beauté*, he was called by de Vogué, when he attempted to enter Parliament). In the war however, he proved himself a man of action who later, for many months, defied powerful governments. He joined the Air Force in the hope of achieving immortality, even at the cost of his life. In one flight he lost an eye; in another he was wounded in the wrist. He led a propaganda flight over Vienna, showering that city with pamphlets. On more occasions than one his plane was riddled with bullets. Later he changed elements and, as a submarine commander, torpedoed five enemy vessels in Bucari Harbour.

He became a sort of uncrowned king of Fiume in 1919 when, with his own personal army, he occupied the town for eighteen months, defying even his own Government—who later created him a Duke for this piece of insubordination. Like Nelson's, it was on a big enough scale to make it highly respected. His love affairs are almost as famous in Italy as those of Casanova. This man, of whom an enemy said, "He is a mixture of monkey, mountebank and spoilt child," seems to be a throw-back to an Italy we know only from the history books.

Masceri had, as usual, some stories about the sanguinary adventures that had taken place in Anversa. He knew that I wanted to meet a bandit; in fact, he was convinced that this was my only reason for coming to Italy. And, with truly Italian imagination, allied to truly Italian desire to please, he never failed to give me vivid pictures of the bandits, robbers and other criminals he had known, or claimed to have known, in his *patria*.

"There," he had said as we were nearing Anversa, "there on the hillside, in that farm, is a man who would interest you. A most respectable fellow now. But who, only three years ago, was wanted for murder. And up there in Villalago is another for you, a baker who burnt his wife alive. I could give you a list of them. In Scanno, I know a soldier who shot his best friend. *Affare d'amore*, of course. . . ."

It was during my last morning in Anversa that I met the bandit he had promised me. He went to fetch this man and said he would bring him at midday to the fountain near the main piazza, where I was to meet him.

This gave me an excuse for doing, this last morning while waiting, something I have always wanted to in Italy—to make a point of speaking to *everyone* who came up to the fountain, a sentence, a phrase, a word—anything to obtain a response: from the urchins who came to loiter and throw in stones; from the old men who came to *chiacchierare*; the young women who came to fill their pots.

Many, like the urchins, had little to say, and replied to my *buon giorno* either with a stony stare or with some noncommittal remark. But at last an old man, smelling strongly of garlic, approached. He surveyed me for some time.

"*Giovanotto*," he said at length, "I have been watching you. You are standing there like a sentinel. Are you by any chance a journalist?"

"Not exactly," I said.

"A foreigner?" he said quickly.

"I am English," I said.

"An Englishman! Well, I never!" For some seconds he remained stupefied. "And what on earth might an Englishman be doing here? In Anversa degli Abruzzi! Englishmen, the most learned, the most intelligent, the most cultured people in the world! What can you find in a place that has neither literature, science, art, nor indeed anything of the remotest interest?"

"I find it most interesting," I said.

"Anversa! Why, it is the most benighted place on earth! If it were not for my work, I would not stay here a second longer. I can tell you this, for I have lived six years in Kansas City. I know your wonderful civilisation."

"I am not an American," I said.

"Well, an Englishman, then," he said loftily. "Why"—he returned to his first question—"do you speak to everyone who comes to the fountain if you are not a journalist? You are too young to be a philosopher."

"I am curious," I said. "I want to hear what they have to say."

He stared at me incredulously for some seconds. "Well, let me tell you you are wasting your time here," he said gruffly. "They have nothing to say, these people! Nothing! Absolutely nothing! These idiots!" And with that he stumped away. I was sorry to see him go, for he might have had much to say himself.

I waited another half an hour, until after midday, and was about to go off to lunch, thinking Masceri and his bandit had forgotten me, when I saw another man approaching. He came right up, stared rudely, hiccoughed and then said, "English Captain, your muleteer is drunk."

I remembered that Masceri had said the bandit he was meeting was an old Army friend whom he had not seen for some years. This man's words might well be true. They had perhaps been "celebrating".

"Yes; he is dead drunk," he continued complacently. "And is now on his way to find you, under the impression you are an English Captain."

He smelt strongly of alcohol himself, and I asked if they had been together. He tipped his nose in the air and said, "Exactly. We have. The English Captain is right."

He then came up again right under me, in an almost menacing manner; and then, when I thought this drunkard was about to strike me, he suddenly narrowed his eyes and pointed down the road. "Here! Quick!" he said. "Stand aside! He is coming!" And he drew me hastily under the arch.

Down the road came Masceri. He was certainly the worse for drink. Some dark memory no doubt still told him that he was supposed to come to the fountain at midday, for he lumbered up, stared at it with unseeing eyes for about ten seconds and then started in a low voice to sing "God Save the King." He did not notice us, uttered some more incoherent nonsense in English and then lurched away.

"He tells me," hiccoughed the man, "that you want to meet a bandit. Well, I am your man."

"*You*, a bandit!" I said to this repellent drunkard.

"I was," he said. "I have been two years in the island of Procida. In the penitentiary."

"And what," I asked, "was your crime?"

"I sold dope to the American boys in Naples," he said proudly. "In 1943. If you like, I'll tell you about it." He pointed to the café.

I had nothing to do, so I took him in. For a drink, he was prepared to tell me all about his misdeeds—which were very far from the banditry I had hoped to hear of. Among other things he had stolen a consignment of American Army clothing, and sold it on those stands you see in every Italian market-place —woollen caps, khaki sweaters, gas-capes, beige underwear, battledress tunics. I left him ten minutes later without enthusiasm. Gone were the Italian bandits of my boyhood dreams! The bearded ruffians, sitting round an enormous fire fed by the trunk of a cork tree, eating fricasseed rabbit and olives and drinking the muddy but fiery wine. Such people now steal, perhaps even wear, American Army combinations, like myself.

CHAPTER THIRTEEN

The Town of the Beautiful Women

FREQUENTLY IN ITALY you will find a street with the name, *Via delle Belle Donne*. There is one in Florence, another in Aquila, and in many of the smaller towns of central Italy. It seems to have the same frequency as the French *rue d'Austerlitz* or the English *Station Road* (and as such, says something perhaps about the character of those peoples).

About twenty miles from Anversa up the valley of the Sagittario, lies the little village of Scanno, renowned throughout Italy for the beauty of its women, the *città delle belle donne*, situated beside a small lake of the same name, with waters so emerald that they recall an Alpine scene. The height above sea-level is no doubt responsible for this; for the lakes of central Italy are normally stagnant, miasmic waters, motionless mirrors, like Trasimene or Bolsano, where the air one breathes at sundown is dangerous. But here, surrounded by oaks and chestnuts, on the last stages of the journey as we climbed ever higher, the air became fresh and balsamic. We might have been by the waters of the Inn, in the latitude of the Engadine—not of the Pontine Marshes, only eighty miles away.

The guide-book makes extravagant claims for these damsels, who it says are descended from the Saracens. This in itself would hardly recommend them, one would think. But it is impossible to deny their charm, poise and dignity. We saw a number of them standing near a fountain when we arrived and I examined them closely. They are dark; they are brown; they are black-eyed, with beautiful firm eyebrows; their teeth are sound and their smile is sweet. They carry things on their head, the most unlikely objects—bundles of wood, sacks of grass, bales of linen, copper tubs with the wash, barrels of wine. Thus their hands are left free to carry baby or knit a stocking. It is apparently entirely against the tradition to carry your baby on your head.

Their traditional costume is of the fifteenth century, and to see them in their marriage dress is the aim of every photographer of Italian antiquities. A blue turban with gold or silver bands is placed at a provocative angle on the head. A bodice of broadcloth studded with filagreed ornamental buttons covers a thin chemise of *petit-point* muslin. The plaited skirt is so heavy that it is held from the shoulders by bands. Beneath it is the corset, as hard as saddle leather, which holds up the breasts, like some sort of mediæval cuirass, as if to guard their virtue—a solid rampart which also frequently serves as a pocket. Around their necks hang heavy coral necklaces and golden chains, and their ears are heavy with rosettes of pearls. Bangles and heavy circular earrings complete the appearance of these birds of paradise.

The people of Scanno, unlike those of almost every other village we had stayed in, appeared accustomed to strangers. They never stared. And two of the girls in these ceremonial dresses on Sunday said they would gladly pose for a photograph. In a picturesque corner of the village, on the polygonal *pavé*, I took them, with a chicken. They had sombre, sad expressions and one of them, who always insisted on remaining in profile, had Greek features and beautiful almond-shaped eyes. That they did this frequently for tourists was clear, for they quickly adopted stereotyped positions, while a number of older women clustered around, arranging their frills and flounces, making sounds of excitement and pleasure, like hens at the approach of spring. It appeared that they took me for an American.

That afternoon I was seated at the fountain, hoping for another photograph, when a lissom girl appeared. She could not have been more than eighteen and was of a truly admirable grace, with the most luscious, liquid black eyes I have ever seen. At first I thought I might be able to talk to her and photograph her; but then I saw she had only come to drape herself elegantly on the parapet for a young man, equally graceful and also with liquid black eyes who, from twelve yards away, was taking a photograph too! I moved aside, so that she should be left alone in the sunlight with the stone Neptune and the cupids emitting jets of water.

"Please do not move!" cried the young man peremptorily, looking down into his camera.

"But you don't want *me* in the photo?" I said.

"Stay!" cried the girl, indicating that I should sit beside her. And she explained that this was her brother, who was a professional photographer making a series of calendar pictures, which they would sell. "We make our living like this," she said.

"If he is as excellent a photographer as you are a model," I said, posing beside her, "you must make a pretty good living."

She smiled sweetly; the camera went click. And I suppose I am now hanging up over somebody's fireplace, above the month of May.

I learned later that this young lady was not a *Scannese* at all! She and her brother were Romans, who went round Italy dressing up and photographing one another in whatever costume or setting would make a pretty picture. One day she would be the Venus of Medici; the next, Diana; then Ariadne, or the Holy Virgin; a bacchante; a slave; a martyr in the Coliseum; one day completely nude, the next clothed in the thickest satins of Ghirlandaio's Tuscan ladies. But in the photograph with me she looked, I thought, quite Roman—one of those nymphs perhaps who used to inhabit the Tarpeian rock.

The scenes on the streets in the evening of the beautiful *Scannese* women in dalliance with the gorgeous *Carabinieri* in their off-duty hours were not quite those I had been led to expect from the guide-book: ". . . girls with the mystic thyrsus engarlanded by vines, with torches, singing the local lullabies of love to the *mélopée* of the flute and the bagpipe. . . ."

They seemed, once out of their beautiful costume, like normal twentieth-century women. And I reflected that, in spite of all their charm, I am still a northerner at heart. The English are still, to me, the champions of feminine beauty. We produce a small, a restricted vintage, it is true; but it is of the highest quality. Out of 100 Italian women, you will find as many as seventy that are charming, cute, *graziose*, even pretty; but only one that is beautiful. Out of 100 English women thirty will be plain; twenty not too bad, if a trifle graceless; forty definitely grotesque. But ten are of a beauty fallen, it seems, from the skies— with a freshness, an innocence, a grace which no quick-eyed Latin can ever attain.

CHAPTER FOURTEEN

Pilgrims

AFTER SCANNO WE turned due west towards
Rome, cutting transversely across the mountains
—a land of parallel ranges enclosing valleys and basins;
at the end of each, a town or village administering the
soil within its basin, as much removed from its neighbours as scattered townships in adjacent valleys of
the Alps. These chains and spurs which divide the
Sulmona area from the basin of |Fucino, run parallel
or touch and intersect in a maze of rock thrown up by
Nature in her sudden cataclysm, a land of peak and
pit, of ravine and mamelon—but with those sudden
surprises of which only the south is capable. Suddenly
the wilderness blooms beside a stream, and what
seemed a block of burnt and calcined granite proves
to be the wall that guards a cloister—within, a garden
of vines and fruit trees, wistaria and banksia falling in
thick masses, Judas trees ablaze against the summer
sun.

The weather was fine but not too hot, and we were
generally on the road by sunrise, without any incon-
venience to a sluggish person like myself. This early
rising may shock some people. But something in Italy
always makes me want to get up with the dawn. In
England, this is not so. Perhaps I am sleepier there,
I don't know. I haven't seen a British sunrise for
years, and have little wish to do so. But here, in rural
Italy, in this burning climate, the freshness of the
early hours is invigorating. Innumerable smells, from
earth, bush and flower, assail one, and every morning

I saw the dawn in a new setting; across the mysterious valleys and infolding Sabine hills; above great bare rocks on the Monte Bove Pass; and over the white surface of the Valerian Way that went winding across it. And then, finally, above the city itself, in Rome, when the white-frocked monks and pilgrims of San Clemente in procession, chanted their wonderful Latin dirge.

As we approached Rome, this atmosphere of Holy Year and its pilgrims began to make itself felt. (I considered myself, in a sense, a pilgrim, for I wanted to see the Pope at the end of our journey, and I hoped to meet fellow-pilgrims on the way.) But it was not until now, just above Cucullo, that we came upon our first group, real, serious ones, carrying a cross, having come all the way from Dalmatia on foot— just as their predecessors had been coming every Holy Year for the last six centuries.

For the belief that, by visiting the tombs of the saints or places where they have lived in Holy Year, one would be invested with some of their virtue, is an old one. The Christian shrines of Europe—Rome, Vezelay, St. Jacques de Compostella—have, almost since pilgrimages began, attracted people from the ends of the Continent. And Rome of all places, with her precious relics—the wood of the True Cross, the Sudario, the Scala Santa, the Column of the Flagellation, and above all the tombs of Peter and Paul—has always offered this facility more than any other shrine in Christendom.

We came upon these men and women on a rough track in the hills. They were carrying a large wooden cross and singing songs, clearly of a spiritual nature, melancholy and monotonous like the *stornello* of a monk. We overtook them and I noted that three men were actually carrying the cross, while the rest walked beside, about a dozen, of whom four were monks.

I asked one of the laymen where they had come from, and he replied, pointing to the monks, that they had come from Dalmatia. It amazed me that men should come so far, on foot, carrying such a burden!

"But *they* don't carry it," he said, pointing to the monks again. And he explained that a pilgrimage of this kind is arranged months beforehand; that the actual pilgrims—in this case the four Dalmatian monks —never carry the cross themselves. At each town or village where they arrive on the way, local enthusiasts turn out and do the carrying for them, until the next town or village, where it is taken over by another set of locals. It was now, for the first time, that I felt the nearness of Rome.

We continued with them for a short time until, at a village *trattoria*, they stopped. The cross was rested against the wall, and everyone went in for refreshment. The Calvary seemed less grim than I had imagined. But all the same, it is some feat to come all the way from Dalmatia on foot.

In the Middle Ages, when the pilgrimages started, to come on foot was obligatory, of course. The journey was then long (ninety days from Paris). And many dropped by the way, from exhaustion or the violences they received; or, in extreme cases, even reaching Rome, and then falling beneath the blows of the Devil, who lay in wait up a nut-tree outside the gates, above the grave of Nero.

But nothing discouraged the faithful, and the pilgrimages never flagged. That the dangers were considerable is shown by the habit most pilgrims had, before setting out, of making their wills—for the Saracens were still marauding and often carried some away to North Africa. Not the least of their troubles was the custom of the time, by which municipalities levied taxes on all foreigners entering their walls; or, if they were moneyless, of simply locking them up as vagrants (one poor Parisian pilgrim remaining in Siena, "on bread and water in a dripping dungeon for a space of three years")—and this in spite of the Pope's injunction that all pilgrims should be exempted from taxation, and given free lodging in the monasteries and convents! A wealthy Dane left his fortune to the towns of Piacenza and Lucca, for all pilgrims of his nationality to be provided with wine free of charge. Of course there were a good many impostors, pilgrims who were really, like ourselves, only glorified tramps.

It was in a convent that I had another meeting with pilgrims, some days later. We had spent the night in a wayside inn, where I had been literally devoured alive by vermin. I was heartily looking forward to leaving the next morning, when Pepe the donkey made an extraordinary sound from his nostrils—a cross between a sneeze and that type of frenzied love-greeting with which donkeys greet one another from afar. This was followed by a fit of violent trembling; and then out of his nostrils came a noise like a volley of small-arms fire, which went on into a sort of crescendo, until I thought he was going to explode.

"He has it," said Masceri professionally.

"Has what?" I asked.

"Heart trouble," he said. "And now it has gone to his head."

I knew Pepe was an elderly donkey, but I didn't understand how this complication could set in. However, I did not argue when Masceri said there was no question of leaving that day; for the animal was clearly in pain. Masceri said he would have to give him an oil-bath. And I later saw him doing this, rubbing the donkey all over with olive oil (rather, I remember, as my grandmother used to rub my chest with camphorated oil when I was small, and had a cold). I watched for a while and then, deafened by the unending sternutations of Pepe—which the oil seemed to aggravate rather than diminish—I left, and spent the morning wandering despondently round the village in search of other billets.

It was a dark, dreary place, even under the Mediterranean sun, with narrow alleys and sharp, sudden climbs between the blackened buildings huddling round the trecento church. In the only place that resembled a *trattoria*, I asked the slatternly *padrona* if she had a spare bedroom.

"We had one once," she said sadly, "but the Germans blew it up."

"I find it rather strange," I said bitterly, "that they should have blown up just the room which a wanderer like myself might inhabit. Why did they not blow up *your* room, for example? Indeed, the whole building?" I was now becoming annoyed about the difficulties I was always having with rooms.

"The Germans would have done so, I assure you," she said, "had they been able. But they were retreating, and they had only enough explosive for one room. So, naturally, they chose the largest."

"Well, at least give me some advice about the rest of the village," I said.

"There is nothing, absolutely nothing," she said. "We have been reduced to *la miseria* by the war and the Government. No one except honourable persons like yourself ever comes our way. Not even commercial travellers. Stay! No! Wait!" She placed her finger to her lips. "I had forgotten. Of course, it is Holy Year. The nuns in the convent have said they will lodge all pilgrims. Are you a pilgrim?"

"Yes," I said determinedly.

"Well," she said, "you must go to the big convent just outside the town . . ." and she gave me instructions about finding it.

Accordingly, that afternoon I found myself approaching a large four-square building to the north of the town, from the inside of which came sounds of singing. At the door sat a little old woman, counting over 5- and 10-*lire* notes at a desk, shuffling them as if they were playing-cards. She seemed some sort of *concierge*.

"*Signora*," I said, "I understand in the town that you are kindly providing accommodation for pilgrims. I am benighted. I and my muleteer. Can you lodge us to-night?"

"Wait, wait!" she said busily. "Can you not see that I am treasurer?" And she went on shuffling the money.

(Can I, I thought, stepping back and looking up, have come to the right place? For I had seen from my guide-book that there was a lunatic asylum just outside this village.)

At length, however, she finished and put on a pair of spectacles, through which she peered at me. "A male!" she said at last.

"That is my sex, *signora*," I replied. "Does that prevent my staying here? I am of a serious, orderly nature and shall spend the whole night in profound sleep, of which I am in great need. My muleteer also, a man from these parts, is well-behaved. *È una persona seria*."

"The Little Sisters have never refused hospitality to a pilgrim for five hundred years," she said. "This is open house in 1950. But you must sleep in the barn, for we have a group of French pilgrims to-night. Hark! You can hear them singing now!" She raised her finger, and from one of the windows above there floated down the most disagreeable sounds.

"Sign your name and nationality here," she said.

It was not the first time in Italy I had thankfully accepted a barn; and so I signed my name.

"Can you sing?" she asked.

"No," I replied. "Why?"

"Because we are in need of a male voice for the *Stabat Mater*, which they are now singing. Listen!"

She again held up her finger, and a look of seraphic calm suffused her ugly face.

"But if I remember correctly," I said, "that is by Pergolesi. And it is for female voices alone."

"That is so," she said. "But the French women pilgrims have brought three husbands with them. And they are most anxious that the men shall take part too. They are forming a quartet. You would make"—she looked me up and down—"an—er—an addition. . . ."

(She could hardly say more, I was aware; for I was not looking my best. Upon my head I wore a hat which appeared to have been trodden underfoot; a rusty-coloured shirt, which had served, my mother had told me, my grandfather, enwrapped me; my trousers were well covered with mud, which also bespattered my face, upon which was a three days' growth of beard.)

"The Mother Superior," she continued, "has been asking in the village for another male voice. You will have to help." And she began counting her money again.

After such hospitality it seemed churlish not to, particularly as I had nothing to do for the rest of the day. So I said I would, but that my voice was most unmusical.

"That," she said, "is of the smallest importance. Those Frenchmen cannot sing. Listen!"

The female voices had now stopped and a truly astonishing sound was floating down, not unlike the sneezing of our donkey, Pepe.

"No!" I said. "That is an animal."

"Precisely," she said. "The male animal."

And with that she led me upstairs. I said I must wash first. She took me to a closet, where I shaved and cleaned myself. She then returned and I was escorted to the singers.

I found myself in a large *aula* or hall, in which was a choir of about thirty nuns and some women in lay

dress. Opposite, in a minority which made me understand the need for my presence, stood three small and
hairy men. All were holding musical scores and singing
at the top of their voices. At the end of the room stood
an elderly woman who might have been the Mother
Superior had she not resembled in almost every
particular, my idea of Mistress Quickly. Tall, bony and
shrewish, she was beating time with a stick, long,
heavy and more suitable, I should have thought, as an
instrument of punishment than a conductor's baton.
On seeing me, she made a sharp upward movement
with it. And silence fell.

"Let the newcomer stand to the right," she said
sharply, pointing to the Frenchmen. "Give him a
score. Does he know the Latin language?"

"A little," I said guardedly.

"Capital! Let us hope he can pronounce it better
than our friends here."

The Frenchmen looked at their boots; and some of
their womenfolk tittered.

"Silence!" said the Mother Superior with a voice
like thunder. A silence fell on the room again.

I now began to feel quite frightened and said involun-
tarily, "*Madre*, my voice is very uneven. I think I had
better go."

"You will go," she said, "when we have finished."

I took my place beside the Frenchmen.

The female singers now struck up. Pergolesi was,
one might say, flayed alive. Not a note of that beautiful
work was spared. We passed through the entire score.
Now, I can read music; I once played second clarinet
in an amateur orchestra, with many squeaks and
squeals and with pleasure only to myself. But my
clarinet-playing, compared with my singing, is a dulcet
thing.

"What is your nationality?" said Mistress Quickly,
when she heard me.

"English," I said.

"Let the Englishman try a scale alone."

This I did, as well as I could.

"Let the Englishman stand aside," she said, "until the big chorus."

And so it went on, for nearly two hours—until I felt I had more than earned my night's rest. In this large hall, hung with tapestries, surrounded by the gold and silver ornaments of the Catholic Faith, I warbled and tremoloed in the company of three perspiring Frenchmen and their wives, until my vocal chords were red hot. At this point, when I thought I would collapse, Mistress Quickly said mercifully to the Frenchmen, "That will do for to-day. You may go. Monsieur Birmélé, your wife has, I can see, taught you something. Monsieur Montoux, I have little to add to what I said last night. Monsieur Rappard, you have not got rid of your cold. Of the Englishman I will say nothing. He is no doubt tired."

We were now dismissed. The husbands were united to their wives; me to Masceri; while Mistress Quickly went into conference with another tall and angular person of indeterminate sex who emerged from behind the piano.

After dinner, I found myself closeted for the night with one of the Frenchmen. They were not allowed to sleep with their wives; and we had been allotted a sort of attic in the barn, with cubicles, each containing two beds. My companion was M. Rappard. He was large and self-confident and clearly not accustomed to such quarters. He came from Dijon and, as befitted a man from the Côte D'Or, spoke with great scorn of Italian food—indeed, of things Italian in general. It appeared that he had never wanted to make this pilgrimage to Rome. His wife had insisted on it. They had come by car (a large American car which I later saw), but it had broken down in this ghastly little village and it would take at least three days to get the spare parts. He made no overt reference to his wife, but I suspected that his diatribe against Italy and the Italians was connected in some obscure way with this buxom, cacophonous woman whom I had heard singing, for he said bitterly, when we were in bed:

"Your Italian, if you are polite and sociable towards him, will show you his thanks by making love to your wife, if she is beautiful."

I made no attempt to defend the Italians on this score; neither did I mention that this is precisely the attitude of my countrymen towards *his* race, the French! Instead, I remarked that I had been married myself, and that this was exactly the impression I had received of the inhabitants of a number of other countries; and that if he felt so strongly about it he had better be careful where he went. "All peoples," I said pontifically, "can be accused of that from time to time, I expect. Adultery is, after all, not an exclusively Italian habit. I fear you are being subjective."

I heard him moving in his bed with some warmth. "Are you insinuating that I am referring to my *own* wife?" he said. "Nothing of the kind! I was merely making a general observation. Do you mean to say *your* wife cuckolded you?"

"Certainly not," I said. "It was a figure of speech. I too was making a general observation."

And with that we turned our backs on one another and went to sleep.

I ate my meals the next day with this man and his friends. They had found the only passable restaurant in the place which, in all my previous wandering, I had been unable to discover. M. Rappard thought little of it, however. And with its narrow tables, wine-stained napkins, smells of dried fish and people in shirt-sleeves, it was impossible not to treat it (to use his words), as a *pis aller*.

The waiter, flattered perhaps by the sudden cosmopolitan society, recited the menu at lunch in the most horrible polyglot jargon I have ever heard, even in Italy. "*Macaroni al graten, patate masche, entrecots, gulasch, bifsteak. . . .*" He boasted to the Frenchmen that here, in his restaurant, was the *cucina francese*. Now everyone prefers French cooking, it is true, but the results this man had achieved were not happy. In his attempts to create tasty sauces, the meat smelt of fish, the fish of mushrooms, the vegetables of wine and the wine of soup.

As I ate and listened to my grumbling companions, male and female, I thought how unattractive can be the Latin race in its modern brands. When the average Englishman thinks of the average Frenchman, is it not generally of an ill-dressed, dirty little waiter, the chief thing about him being the word *undistinguished*? But it is these Latins (with their Italian cousins) who have given us everything worth having in our civilisation. Is there anything more one can ask from the map of the world than France and Italy? Between the Straits of Dover and Messina I will gladly live and die.

But as I looked at these fat Frenchmen with their wives, truffling away, I thought that it was a Frenchman, too, Stendhal, who said of Italy: "*En ce beau pays, il n'y à rien a faire que l'amour.*" These people seemed as far away from *that* sort of love as you could get. For when I am in Italy and think of Love, it is in the most extravagantly romantic terms—the Apollo of Belvedere in the arms of the Venus of Medici, in some whispering garden of Posillipo—not a gross Lillois on his Flamande in a grubby Roubaix *rez-de-chausée*.

As if divining these uncharitable thoughts, one of the Frenchmen turned to me at the end of the meal and delivered a sort of homily against the Anglo-Saxons who, he said, had at all times been selfish and deceitful; but that their present conduct towards France—indeed, towards all Europe—was particularly deplorable. For though we could easily put a stop to the present political troubles in Germany by sending a good general and a large force, we preferred to contribute a handful of troops officered largely by American Negroes, in order that the present disagreeable situation might be prolonged, simply because it was to our advantage to have France economically weak.

Not being well-informed in politics, I had some difficulty in combating this statement. But I tried. "Do you, then," I said, "count among our selfish actions the stirring events of 1944 when we, together with the Americans, sent fifty *white* generals and at least 500,000 troops, and liberated your continent from a hateful yoke?"

"What matter," said M. Rappard bitterly. "Another yoke, a worse one, is about to descend upon us. And *you* brought it about."

With such churlishness I did not attempt to argue. And that evening I said goodbye to this cynical pilgrim.

CHAPTER FIFTEEN

The Reclaimed Lake

WE NOW ARRIVED at the edge of the vast agricultural basin which was once the lake of Fuçino. Where half the corn of Central Italy now waves was once a sluggish inland sea, breeding malaria, typhoid and other paludal ills. In the winter it had the appearance of a sea of asphodel; but in summer it became a Tartary—like the Pontine Marshes, so unhealthy that not even the murderer was followed when he had taken refuge here.

All this has been transformed within the lifetime of living man—the lake drained, the plain planted, acres of marshland reclaimed. To come across the barren mountains where we had been travelling and see below this Canaan leaves an unforgettable impression. Suddenly before one is a vision of Italy as she must have been, almost of classical times, the Italy of the *Georgics*, with "the sensuous beauty of ripening wheat and vineyard," Italy, "the mother of crops and men".

That this vision of Fucino is no chimerical dream is clear from the number of rulers who, throughout the centuries, have appreciated its agricultural possibilities and contemplated draining it. Julius Cæsar, Claudius, Marcus Aurelius, various Renaissance Popes; they all, at one time or another, formed grandiose projects for doing so. Cæsar came nearest to it with a huge aqueduct he planned, for taking all the water down to the sea somewhere near Rome. The Ides of March and the civil disturbances that ensued prevented the execution of this. Claudius had a complicated plan for employing slave labour, but his energies were also diverted from the social services. Certain Popes, dependent upon the degree of security prevailing in Rome at the moment, contemplated it, but generally found that military obligations deflected them. The task in those days would have required at least twenty-five years of peace—an unheard-of stretch of tranquillity. Napoleon, needless to say, was also attracted by the idea.

It was therefore left to the modern engineering methods of Alessandro Torlonia to realise the 2,000-year-old project. He agreed to sink his entire fortune in it in 1880, if he could obtain certain rights and concessions in the area afterwards. He had to fight hard against Nature; so that people betted whether "Torlonia would drain Fucino, or Fucino would drain Torlonia". Torlonia won; after ten years and many setbacks, he drained it. And for his pains he was created a Prince—presumably the only case in history of a man being made a prince for draining a lake.

His family now live in Rome in fabulous state on the proceeds, a constant butt for Communist propaganda; for in some ingenious Italian way, he has contrived that he and his descendants shall be for ever exempted from taxation, enjoying, it is said, an income of half a million pounds a year. But whatever the present abuses, the peasants have not forgotten that it was Torlonia who drained Fucino and abolished *il Paludismo*.

Our arrival in this Canaan coincided, appropriately, with a village *festa*. A row of very small female children, dressed as angels, in almost nothing but wings and flowers, each clasping a lily, welcomed us as we entered the town on our donkey. The clanging of bells, the exploding of maroons, the trumpeting of a brass band, indicated that the Catholic Church was organising something. All the *campanili* of the district seemed to be ringing in antiphon. The piazza was crammed with people in black, many of whom were also buying at market stalls.

It was impossible to make any headway through this, so Masceri tied the donkey to what appeared to be a stall, and we sat down to drink at a nearby table. It was only then, on seeing the stall from the front, that I realised it was a Punch and Judy show, in full work, surrounded by vociferating children; and the donkey had only to stampede to pull the whole thing to pieces. But I should, by now, have known Pepe better. He had a stolidity passing all comprehension. If one of the explosives had been let off right under him, he would I am sure, have subsided quite gently without making a sound. Interior, not exterior, excitements ruled the behaviour of our donkey.

After lunch a lull descended on all this piazza activity; and everyone went off this stifling afternoon for a *siesta*. That favourite occupation of the Italian race, to stand in the street and talk, was replaced by that other one—to sleep. It was too hot even to sit inside the café and be consumed by flies, so I entered the church where all this excitement had been taking place. And immediately, that wonderful coolness of the Italian church in summer possessed me. The heavy leather curtain is pulled aside, and one plunges in from a burning piazza, to meet a cool draught of incense-laden air.

In this vast cathedral-like church, out of all proportion an Englishman would say, to the size of the village it served, a host of activities still seemed to be going on. At one end, High Mass was being bawled and drawled by some priests, to the accompaniment of an asthmatic organ with a painted fretwork frame. Around them, racked and distorted Christs and death-heads, by which pilgrims were praying or hanging votive gifts, of silver hearts, old crutches and bandages, told eloquently of the reason for it all.

It is difficult to say, when one watches an old cripple woman kneeling to one of these Christs—an expression of suffering, supplication and pity for the Saviour on her face—who is really in pain. A Frenchman has said that the Italians depict Christ suffering so that they can pity *Him*, not He *them*. The emaciated features, the bleeding ribs, the contorted muscles, the gaping mouth, the straggly hair, the sweaty brow, the head that barely holds its wreath of thorns—such a Christ clearly cannot aid another sufferer. But He knows all pain, as we do; and His sacrifice, as such, is more companionable than vicarious.

I had been in this church about half an hour when a sacristan came up and offered to show me round. Although something in his manner told me that he clearly did this for a tip (he treated his own Church as a spittoon), I had nothing to do, so I thanked him and followed him. He had a large face, almost quadrangular, two eyes the size of a mouse's; yawning nostrils, and wiry hair which rose vertically on his forehead like a hog's bristle—in appearance more suitable, I should have thought, to a brewery than a basilica. He took me through a cloister and into a library, which also served as a sort of museum, where he discoursed volubly on various works of art—but with that plausibility, I suspected, which often takes the place in Italy of accuracy.

"We have here," he said, "many examples of the work of our local artists, in particular of the Renaissance period. . . ."

In this dirty little village, under the guidance of this man who probably always has two weeks' growth of beard on his chin, neither more nor less, it was wonderful to think of the richness of Italy. Even here, there is beauty! I catalogue the more picturesque of the exhibits he showed me, if only because they are representative of what is to be found in almost every church or museum, however mean, in this wonderful land:

I

A mediæval warrior, fallen and defending himself; a Græco-Roman satyr playing a flute; Cupid sharpening an arrow; Hercules strangling a lion (this, a very decadent piece of work); a Roman matron intoxicated, or so it seemed; the head of the Imperial sadist Nero, the strain of violent mental tension on his brow. And then, the usual rather dull selection of hagiographic bric-à-brac.

Most people, I suppose, come to Italy to-day to see this sort of thing—a mad rush from church to church, from city to city, from work of art to work of art; to see Tintoretto's *Virgin enthroned between Mars and Neptune*; or a group representing Faith in the act of converting a Japanese; or Religion destroying Heresy —before which one cries, "*Che bellezza!*" or alternatively "The one in Siena has more nervous chiaroscuro". Then on to the next clerico-artistic demonstration.

When I had seen all, I thanked him and gave him 200 *lire* for his pains. He promptly began to ask for more, saying that the English and Americans were always the most benevolent of visitors. It would have been the same if I had given him 2,000 *lire*, I am sure. A sudden fit of fury with all Italians who offer unasked-for services in return for tips taken without gratitude took hold of me. I refused churlishly and went out into the piazza.

Yet even here, on the marble steps, sat a beggar, displaying his misery to view, showing the whites of his eyes and holding out his hat! The works of art I had just seen, together with this beggar and the sacristan, seemed expressive not only of the land and its treasures, but also of the people. Incalculably rich in art, her every village bursting with priceless master-pieces, Italy is an impecunious sacristan, grasping the riches with one dirty hand, the other extended for alms.

The streets were still silent, the heat oppressive with the dampness of the dried-up lake, the faces that

I passed pale, as if with some ancient fever. And I suddenly felt an intense desire to leave this land where death and decay linger and where everything speaks of the past. Even the carved doorways, with their ancestral *stemme*, confirmed the legends of former greatness, when *signori* lived here centuries ago.

In this mood, as I stepped into the piazza, I was greeted by a singing voice—but such sounds as to make the blood course within me! Outside a small wickermender's shop on the corner, a man was singing as he worked—that *bel-canto* of the Italian tenor, which seems to come to you from some distant, echoing cave, as if he were singing beneath a rock, with a catch in his throat at the end of each phrase. A voice more troubling than the Lorelei's! In an instant, as I stopped to listen, gone was all my anger. Suddenly I heard and felt Italy again, the Italy of my imagination; a Pintoricchio scene, of ducal citadels and dare-devil *banditti*, of fertile plains crossed by vine-laden trees, of olives, antique ruins and Renaissance glory, blue sky and vivacious manners. In this voice was something too of the great Bay, the *barcarolles* of Naples, always lingering about them the faint odour and mystery of the sea. I sat before a grape-booth and as I listened, drank a dark mahogany-coloured wine that soon clouded my mind with yet more glorious visions of Italy and her past.

CHAPTER SIXTEEN

Tagliacozzo and Alba

ONE OF MY chief reasons for coming to these parts was to visit a very different scene—the battlefield of Tagliacozzo, which lies beneath that town at the extreme western end of this valley.

Why is it, I asked myself the next morning, as I sat in Avezzano (as I have asked myself so many times before), that the scenes of past battles are always so fascinating to me; and those of my own times so dull? Put me in the field of Brixellum near Mantua, where the Emperor Vitellius feasted his eyes on the carnage, and said "The smell of a dead enemy is always sweet" —or at Tagliacozzo in this Sabine vale, where the Hohenstaufen cause in Italy went down before the Angevins—even on some spot where Victor Emmanuel and Garibaldi won their battles-without-tears—and, as I survey the barren plains and dandelions where once the armies pranced, I am enchanted. Yet if you were to *pay* me to go to El Alamein, where the British 8th Army decimated the Italian 108th, I wouldn't.

This explains perhaps why we found ourselves the next morning moving along the Via Valeria as it winds towards the funnel of mountains at the western end of Fucino, towards the town of Tagliacozzo.

Tagliacozzo is so named, because it is situated high in a cut or gap in the side of the hill (*Talus cotium*—the cleavage of the rocks). It is a savage spot—the volcanic hills above, denuded, covered only with asphodel; the windswept mountainside overtopping the little red-roofed town, rather as the mass of Subasio dominates that of Assisi; the steep ascent between the oleanders and the cypress-trees; the fevers from the dried-up marsh waiting, you feel, to assail man should his vigilance relax.

This field marks one of the turning-points in Italian history, like Pavia or Marengo, when the question of who should oppress the Italians for the next 200 years was solved anew. The candidates were, as usual, the French and Germans. But this time the French won and obliterated the energetic House of Hohenstaufen.

On reflection, I think that my real interest in this battlefield lies in its association with the Hohenstaufen. For Frederick II, the father of Conradin, who lost the battle, is one of the few monarchs I like. He attracts to-day because—although cruel and inhumane in the usual mediæval style—the first glimmerings of the Italian Renaissance appear in him. He had a court in Sicily, at which he encouraged poets and musicians, even composing himself; he promised the Pope to go on a crusade against the Sultan in 1190, and set out with an army and the Papal blessing and then, finding the Sultan was quite a pleasant, cultured person, far from having a battle with him, had dinner instead— where they talked about art and mathematics. For this the Pope excommunicated him. (He had obtained the Holy Places by friendly discussion, not by the spilling of blood!)

The Pope now started encouraging the French armies in Southern Italy against him. Frederick was too clever for them during his lifetime; but this Battle of Tagliacozzo where his son lost life and throne to Charles of Anjou, was the belated answer of the Papacy to that hilarious dinner-party in Jerusalem.

I wandered about this field. There is little to say of it. The scenery was like that of fifty other landscapes I had already seen: the barren hillsides enclosing a small plain, the few willows bordering a dried-up stream; some blackened huts in which charcoal-burners and shepherds house their wares; one

or two moth-eaten cypresses. I could not even find a
peasant to talk to. Failing this, while Masceri and
Pepe went to sleep beneath a tree, in the afternoon
heat, I tried to find the "hillock" where the famous
stratagemma which won the battle took place. For
the military historians tell of the clever strategy of
Charles' adviser, Alard de Saint Valéry. They even
refer you to Dante, who mentions this crafty counsellor
in *The Divine Comedy* (Inf. xxviii, 17–18). This man's
clever *stratagemma* was the following:

He recommended that instead of committing all the
French forces to battle, Charles should keep one-third
hidden behind a hillock, on the far side of the stream.
At the crucial moment they would debouch upon the
field, and beat up the Germans from behind. It sounds
simple enough, but it evidently takes a military genius
to think of such a ruse. The effect was instantaneous.
For though, at this moment, things were not going
too well for the French, the tide was immediately
turned, and the Huns put to sudden rout.

Could not, I thought, the German descendants of
those Hunnish Hohenstaufens have remembered this
little lesson at El Alamein?

After the battle the unfortunate young Conradin—
who in character, appearance and destiny seems to
have been as romantic as Bonny Prince Charlie and
the Duke of Monmouth combined—wandered forlornly
about hoping to get away by sea. Disguised as a charming young lady, he and a number of friends at last
found a boat near Anzio on the Tyrrhenian coast.
They were a few hundred yards from land when a
local Italian count called Frangipani, who, like so
many Italian counts throughout history, had calculated
which was the better foreigner to side with, sent out
his ruffians to catch him.

In vain did Conradin plead not to be handed over
to the French King, who was anxious to behead him,

reminding Count Frangipani of all the territory his father had given him. But the benefactor's shade could do nothing against the more tangible benefits this very Italian Italian believed he could obtain from the new victor. Not even Conradin's offer to marry his ugly daughter and make her Queen of the Two Sicilies dissuaded him. The German prince was handed over to Charles of Anjou, who celebrated the victory of Tagliacozzo by beheading the last of the Hohen-staufens in Naples on the 29th October, 1288.

In spite of my enthusiasm for old battles, my chief reason for coming to the Fucino basin was not really to visit this bloody field; not even to admire the handi-work of the Engineer Prince,—but to go out to the pre-Roman site of Alba Fucensis. A friend had spoken enthusiastically about the atmosphere, the *feng-hsui* of these Pelasgic remains. The very word *Alba* fascinated me, meaning "the dawn"—a city which was more important than Rome, almost before history began.

In a landscape of little hills, brown and denuded except for some beech and hornbeam scrub, the ground starred with thistle, we came, the next morning towards midday, upon a small cottage or lodge not far from Avezzano, beside a massive iron gate flanked by pillars, which opened on to an avenue all over grown and unkept. In the heavy iron gate there was a feeling of past greatness, for it was as elaborately worked as gold, an endless invention and imagination; carved Cupids, dolphins and nymphs, arabesques, all arranged into a complex design, now coarse and blackened.

A man who might have been the lodge-keeper was working in the garden in front, and I stopped to ask him if he knew anything about this massive Renaissance gateway, so unusual in the Abruzzi. He replied that it was all that remained of the noble house of della Quercia.

"A mile up that drive," he said, "is a fine ruin. Tourists often come out. Would you like to see it?"

Although his offer was clearly not disinterested, I accepted, and he told me of the signorial house in whose shadow the whole district had flourished and prospered since 1500. He described a castle, surrounded by various annexes, stables, pavilions, lodges, gazebos and other constructions more or less useful. In this house, he said, the family had lived for as far back as anyone could remember. Everything proceeded with perfect order and all the peasants were happy when suddenly, one fine morning fifty years ago—the whole thing caught fire! Within a few hours the place was a pile of ashes! The present Count now lived in Naples; and the countryside, without his patronage, had become a wilderness. There was aristocracy for you, he said! Their domains were now pasture for the shepherd and the swineherd! There was a comment on human fortune!

It was an agreeable saunter to this great, forsaken building, up a clematis-scented hill for about half a mile. I found the castle, as he said, dismantled; a hulk of walls, left to the wild peppermint and caper plants —a species of natural kitchen garden. The old walls that surrounded it, baked yellow by the sun of centuries, still stood, running obstinately up hill and down dale, broken here and there by a cypress grove. Although the inside was completely burnt away, the castle itself still had parts of its towers, mullions and buttresses along the sky-line, with machicolated gates and turrets.

I wondered what its owner, the old Count, was doing now in Naples, divorced from his 500-year-old property. I imagined him as one of those old, cultured, retired noblemen, with which rural Italy is full, dreaming away his days, doing a little archæological digging, or once a month adding a few lines to his work on the ancient Sabines, a book which is never quite ready for the press.

The country around Alba is of peculiar beauty. The land ahead rose to mountainous heights in the Sabines, the view opening out after the watershed we followed to undulating, stony moorlands, high oak forests, dominated everywhere by the last spurs of the mountains. On one of these, now no different from its neighbours, stood once the city of Alba Fucensis, in which the Romans housed their royal captives, the Kings of Numidia and Macedonia. It is now nothing more than a heap of overgrown ruins. In utter abandonment, the land stretches away up into the hills on either side. Here, among the few broken, sporadic columns where priests once sacrificed and worshippers trod, grow the wild parsley, the marigold and the thyme. Temples and baths have gone; wall and amphitheatre are barely recognisable; what survived the Saracens and other barbarians, and various mediæval feuds and pests, has succumbed to earthquake. Of that building fever and passion for luxury of the late Romans which led them to spend vast sums on their country houses—the sumptuous villas, *thermæ*, porticoed swimming-pools—nothing remains.

There is only a sleepy little village of the same name, with goats and sheep nibbling the short grass beneath its walls. We had to pass through it to reach the ancient site, and here, around a group of blackened huts, we came upon some little girls playing in the dirt, bare-footed. One of them was crooning American jazz. She had quite a tuneful voice and, as I had to dismount going through the village, I stopped to listen. Whereupon, she skipped over and proffered a tiny, grimy paw, into which I put a 10-*lire* note. She went on singing all the time; and a feeling of nausea came over me, as I heard the words in broken English on the lips of this babe, ". . . your lips to mine, a kiss like wine . . . honey, hold me tighter in your arms".

To reach the Pelasgic masonry, we walked along a sunken road, between high banks and orchards of vines and eucalyptus trees, lacking the precision of the traditional Roman road, but its origin as a *via* was clearly recognisable in the great uneven slabs of granite, which have resisted the pressure of every kind of vehicle, from the Roman rickshaw to the eighteenth-century carriage—a road that has never known the internal combustion engine. One can walk along it for miles in peace, passing occasionally a flock of sheep or a peasant returning from the fields.

I stopped to ask the way at a farmhouse—if such a name could be given to the hovel outside which two women sat peeling cactus-figs. I was well received, although I could not understand a word of what they said. Fortunately, the owner appeared and offered me a chair under a fig-tree and not only a glass of red, bubbling wine which looked newly fermented, but also a basket of grapes and figs.

"I will gladly show you the wall," he said. "It is in my territory."

What a possession to have in one's "territory"—a wall that was built 800 years before Christ! What English *territorial* magnate, boasting that he and his moated castle date from Angevin times, can compare in richness with this Sabine peasant?

We were by now hungry enough to accept his hospitality and listen to his extremely voluble conversation. We ate and drank freely, while he gave me information and personal opinions about the late war, the present Government, the birth-rate, the taxes. . . . Perhaps the most interesting thing he said was about some Brazilian soldiers who had passed this way during the war, behaving uproariously and immorally. "I knew they must be *Americani*," he said; "they were so *incivili*. They are after all not really Europeans, although they speak Portuguese."

All this he told me in an Italian I could understand. I asked him where he had learnt it, for his womenfolk spoke a southern dialect. The Army, he said, was responsible. Italian was the *lingua franca* of every unit, where the Government deliberately mixed men of all dialects and parts of Italy, to produce a feeling of unity and equality. (An interesting contrast, I thought, with the regionalism of our English county regiments, every one of which is supposed to think it is different from, and superior to, its fellows.)

Dante says in his *De Vulgari Eloquentia*, that the Roman was the ugliest of Italian dialects in 1290. I wondered, as I listened to the two women beside my host, swallowing rather than pronouncing guttural sounds reminiscent of some Dutch peasant, what Dante would have said about this Abruzzi one in 1950. . . .

The man now took me to see the wall. I had heard about the size of these Pelasgic stones, and was prepared for something immense. But this Cyclopean masonry made me suppose that only a race of giants could have placed one stone upon another. They can be compared with the most gigantic constructions of Egypt. Each block is not a square stone, but a veritable rock of irregular shape, weighing tons. Not only is it amazing how they were hoisted, but how they were fitted together, accurately dovetailed so that the interstices are still, to-day, almost invisible.

Little is known about these people, the Pelasgians. Like the builders of Stonehenge, they belong to a prehistoric age. Before their work one feels a sudden admiration for the human race, greater even perhaps than that before the constructions of the Romans— where it is easier to understand how a civilised people, using relatively technical means, could erect the Coliseum and the Pont du Gard. But what did these

Pelasgians know of the crane, the rope, the pulley?
We are told that in those times not even the wheel
existed. Here is surely matter for a university thesis.

In the side of the sunken road, entrances have been
cut to subterranean caverns or *columbaria*, where
funerary hypogea of the ancient Romans were placed,
half-buried beneath mounds of earth and thick, tangled
undergrowth. We descended into one of these and found
ourselves in a sort of ill-lit, smelly crypt, around whose
walls were the niches, "pigeons' nests," about sixty of
them, regularly aligned, each having once held a
cinerary urn, containing the remains of perhaps a whole
family. This was once the cemetery of some equestrian
house. The niches now are empty and full of cobwebs;
and the floor of the tomb was strewn with rubbish of all
kinds, including that most ubiquitous form, excrement.

While we stood there ruminating, a flock of goats
strolled in, in search of shade from the midday sun.
With the air of fully knowing their way about, they
took possession, assuming positions of ease and repose
around the walls, contentedly chewing the cud. Their
shepherd followed and, after a word of greeting to us,
he too settled down beneath one of the *columbaria*,
opened his handkerchief and began to eat.

Thus, the memorials of the Roman patricians, like those
of their Pelasgian forerunners, have accomplished here,
in Alba, the circle of renown and ignominy which
appears to be the lot of civilisations. The Pantheons,
whether of Rome, Westminster or Washington, all
return finally to pasture, to nurture the wandering
herds. And the lines of Horace, in whose country we
were now moving, came into my mind:

"... already the tired shepherd with his languid
    flock looks for the shade and the rill, for the
    windless, silent slope, and the Sylvan thickets
    where the brushwood grows."

CHAPTER SEVENTEEN

The Sabine Farm

TWO DAYS AFTER leaving Avezzano we came to the Aniene, that tributary of the Tiber whose very name tells that this is the land of Horace. The river is spoken of in the guide-books as flowing through wonderful scenery and mountain gorges; but it now seems to have become, for the most part, a series of reservoirs for producing electrical power. There is little to-day of the poet's "hurrying Aniene". Our journey was largely downhill, along the Valerian way of the Legions, now an asphalt surface along which cars and buses flashed by, urgent to reach Rome before nightfall.

Horace's farm is situated about six miles to the north of this road, in the valley of the Licenza, which, at this time of the year, was still in flower—the acanthus with its silver leaves and crimson petals, the pomegranate, the myrtle and the many-coloured bramble lay around us on our path to Licenza. After the flowerless land we had passed over on the Monte Bove Pass, relieved only by a solitary aloe or a cactus plant, the position of this farm in such fertile surroundings well explained the poet's enthusiasm. Whole odes of his later poems are devoted to it. He mentions again and again his *fundus meus*, as if he could never stop thinking about it.

The valley here widens into a kind of natural amphitheatre surrounded by high mountains, all rising to well over 2,000 feet, covered with ilexes and olives and, on the heights, with chestnut-trees. At the foot of one of these, on a little raised plateau, is the farm.

The scene of these hills, with their one narrow portal to the outside world, the Licenza valley, and the richness of the countryside, is well described in one of Horace's letters to his friend, Quintus:

> "*Ne perconteris, fundus meus, Optime Quinti,*
> *arvo pascat erum an bacis opulentet olivæ*
> *pomisne et pratis an amicta vitibus ulmo:*
> *scribetur tibi forma loquaciter et situs agri*
> *Continui montes, ni dissocientur opaca*
> *valle, sed ut veniens dextrum latus aspiciat sol,*
> *lævum discedens curru fugiente vaporet.*
> *Temperiem laudeas. . . ."*[1]

It is possible to quote whole passages of this kind from his letters and odes to establish the Licenza valley topographically as the site. But until quite recently several schools of thought existed. Indeed, throughout the seventeenth and eighteenth centuries, antiquarians were busy arguing or accusing one another of having stolen their ideas about it. A letter written in 1762 by an Italian, de Sanctis, accusing a French *abbé* of this, illustrates this Battle of the Books:

"And after all this, should you by chance hear a certain Ultramontane gentleman, but recently come to Rome, who in 1761 happened to visit Vicovaro with a person of a certain rank, and who then knew no more about the Villa of Horace than he was told and shown by the already mentioned Person—should you now hear him boast pompously of being the discoverer and explorer of the Villa of Horace at Licenza, could you refrain from laughing in his face?"

Whoever was right, one of the chief results of the

---

[1] "I write you at length, my dear Quintus, of the nature and position of my farm, so that you won't have to ask about it. Its owner enjoys its produce and is lucky enough to possess olives, apples, vines and elms in his fields. The hills around are unbroken, save where our valley runs in whose sides, thanks to slanting north and south are continually warm and well-lit, with a temperate climate. . . ."

controversy was to stimulate that interest, already awoken by Winkelmann, for classical remains in Italy; to treat them as something more than mere quarries for obtaining cut stone. And a number of eighteenth-century paintings of the Farm now hanging in the Museum of the nearby village of Licenza, with idyllic shepherdesses reclining on broken columns, and ladies in their powder and panniers on their dandies' arms, bear witness to the new attitude.

All that remains of the Farm to-day are the basement walls of about twenty symmetrically placed rooms. From the top of the little mound to the east they are laid out before you, overgrown with ivy recalling (somewhat sadly to the Londoner to-day) that vision on a larger scale, of the honeycomb behind St. Paul's.

There was a rectangular *patio* to the south enclosing a garden and two central courtyards with covered porticos, where one could walk during the heat of the day; a *Nymphæum* with fountains and a bathing establishment. There are several mosaic pavements which the guardian will uncover, one of which is in the *cubiculum*. Here he indicated the space for a bed. Then, turning to me, he said archly, "He had many friends out here from Rome, you know." I stared at it.

Was this the spot, where Horace made advances to his *dulce ridentem Lalagen?* Was it here that, in the words of Suetonius, he regulated his famous mirrors? "*. . . ad res venereas intemperantior traditur; nam specula toto scortans dicitur habuisse disposta, ita ut quocumque respexisset sibi imago coitus referetur*"?

A point over which there appears to be no argument is that the farm was given to Horace in about 33 B.C. by Mæcenas, who lived in nearby Tivoli. And the poet's gratitude to his rich friend is shown in his later poems and letters. He is glad at last, he says, to get away from the noise and bustle of the city; from its gossips and talk, and the would-be sophisticated set;

he is pleased to be a landowner, even if only on a small scale; to be able to invite friends out from Rome in the hot weather; to enjoy Nature uncloyed by artifice. This love of Nature is to be found in many of his poems—but nowhere perhaps with such delight as in the passages about the Sabine farm:

"O noctes cenæque deum, quibus ipse meique,
ante Larem proprium vescor vernasque procaces
pasco libatis dapibus." [1]

The gardens must have been well-stocked with flowers and statues; and near the villa sparkled the waters of a spring, "fresher and purer than those of the Thracian Hebrus." Some people believe that this was the Bandusian Fount. But the professors, after years of dispute, have established that the famous fountain was near his birthplace, Venosa, in distant Puglia. I walked over to where the waters of this spring mingle on the pebbly falls with the deeper sounds of the Licenza in the valley below. Listening to this water in a wood dedicated to Faunus, Horace says he used to drink beakers of Lesbian wine. Around his vineyard are figs and nut-trees and between the vines, a number of almonds—most precocious tree of the south, flowering with the first warm breezes of the spring. Scabious plants with their pin-cushion flowers abound; golden broom, and the classical acanthus with its Corinthian-shaped leaves and crimson flowers. The experts may have proved that the Bandusian Fount was elsewhere. They can never deny that its *non sine floribus* is confirmed on this Sabine Farm.

Like so many Roman remains, Horace's Farm was later used by the men of the Middle Ages. A number of monks installed themselves here in the eighteenth century. They turned the *patio* into cloisters; and on the site of the *Nymphæum* they

[1] "Before my own hearth I enjoy nocturnal feasts worthy of the gods, and while away both winter and summer with food and wine. . . ."

built a monastery dedicated to St. Marcellinus. Where nymphs and fauns had frolicked, Mass was said. Their mediæval masonry, the coarsely cut blocks of stone and *sperone* which surmount the Latin basement, is clearly distinguishable to-day, almost symbolically, from the neat reticulated brick of classical times.

An attempt has been made since the official recognition of the site as a *monumento nazionale* to lay out the gardens as they were in Horace's day. The paths are overshadowed with myrtle trees, and at each intersection lichen-covered marble busts look down at you forlornly, regretful one might say, of their lost noses. Even now these clipped bushes still have something Roman about them, something of the dying art of the topiarist, by which no tree was allowed to grow in its own way, but was forced into a prescribed form. There were walls of green bay or box with niches, openings and windows, as in an architectural design.

It is not surprising in this countryside, so rich with fruit and flower, that the eloquent guide-book should claim that it was here, in this Sabine vale of Horace and not in Sicily, that Persephone, collecting hyacinths with her girl friends, should have been surprised and carried away by Pluto to the Infernal Regions—whence he allowed her to return to Earth but once a year, bringing with her the phenomenon of Spring. Neither is it surprising that in this land such floral abundance was used in ancient times, as at the feast of the Fontanalia of which Horace tells us in the Bandusian asclepiad, to "crown the fountains and adorn the wells".

At the far end of the grounds is a little coppice of arbutus and mulberry. The word Horace uses for coppice is, to me, one of the most beautiful in his language—*fruticetum*—giving somehow the idea of woodland heavy with fruit and flower—as here on his Sabine Farm.

The restaurant I ate in at the nearby village of

K

Licenza was of a most primitive sort—hardly suitable in the country of an epicure like Horace, who has described some of the luxurious meals he ate on his Farm; the eels and capons, the oysters, the wine flavoured in the Roman way with aloes, myrrh, resin, marble-dust. To enter and leave this dining-room, I had to pass through the kitchen, and here I saw the fertile wench who later brought me my soup, peering over a cauldron. She had a purulent ophthalmia, causing her to wear a crooked bandage over one eye, which was poised 3 inches above the surface of the soup.

At a nearby table sat an ill-dressed fellow who had finished eating and was absent-mindedly picking his teeth and staring at nothing, in the Italian manner. Seeing what I was reading, however (I had felt that there was only one author I could read in Licenza), he immediately came over and began to vouchsafe information. At first I welcomed him, thinking he might be able to tell me something about the poet. He sat at my table and ordered himself a very small cup of black coffee. But he knew little, except that Horace was "a great poet, a very great poet indeed." He repeated this several times; and I realised that his self-introduction was just another way of turning himself into a guide, for he offered to escort me to the Farm after I had eaten.

In many ways, such a spontaneous approach by the Italians is a part of their charm. All they want is to be friendly, act as a guide to something, and then sell you a tinfoil model of it. This man made up for his ignorance too, by tremendous enthusiasm and laughing philosophy, referring to all the great people who had visited the *patria* of Horace—from Napoleon, to Marconi and Stresemann.

"So you're from England, are you?" he said. "England is a great country. And we love England and the English."

But I was in no mood for international amenities. I tried to show him politely that I wished to read the works of his poet. He would not be shown. "From England, eh?" he repeated appraisingly. "From England! Ah!" He shook his finger waggishly, and pointed to the window. "No sun, eh? No sun in England, eh?"

I wondered if he was one of those Italians the President des Brosses speaks of, who are so convinced of England's perpetual fog and rain, that they believe every Englishman goes about with a *portombrella*, a portable umbrella stand, containing instruments for every kind of weather—special sun, rain, hail and snow umbrellas. I explained that I had all the information I required from Giuseppe Lugli's excellent book on the subject, to which, after one or two more amenities, he left me.

In this inn I was allotted for the night what is, I believe, commonly called a *camera interiore*. Most travellers in Italy have at one time or another, I suppose, found themselves in a bedroom whose windows, instead of looking out as windows should, on to the fresh air, do so on to corridors or halls or other parts of the interior—*camera interiori*, cleaned seldom, aired never and possessing their own distinctive aroma—of neither drain, kitchen nor lumber-room, but something of all three.

I am sure, however, that no one has ever been offered, as I was here at Licenza, a *camera interiore* whose one window opened, not on to a corridor or hall—but on to a bathroom-cum-w.c. My rest was disturbed continually by people coming and going to this place; by the light going on and off—until I hated the land of Horace.

CHAPTER EIGHTEEN

A Monastery

ABOUT TWENTY MILES from Horace's Farm, on the other side of the Aniene, the river bends eastward towards its source. And here, in a land of little valleys and rounded hills, stands the town of Subiaco, in which scenes of such violence have taken place as to make even a hardened student of Italian history boggle. Here, where the pious Benedict founded his monastery and order in A.D. 492, the whole tragedy, as well as the comedy, of Italy's 2,000 years has been enacted, on a little stage, almost in miniature. Pope, potentate, abbot, baron, prince, despot and *condottiere* have struggled, murdered, burned, killed, razed, raped and ravaged here, until you might suppose the ground would sprout those tiger-flowers which, the ancients believed, flourished only on a lake of blood. (Art too is, surprisingly, here.)

We arrived one evening in July. The road ascends suddenly and in the sharply indented valley, surrounded by woods of olives, fields of maize and vines that twist from tree to tree, we found ourselves on the last stages of our journey, only thirty miles from Rome, climbing the brown earth towards the oldest Abbey in Christendom. For it was in this wilderness, surrounded by rocky heights burnt by the sun, that the monastic system which spread throughout Italy, France, Germany and England, was born—older even than Monte Cassino, historically more rich.

The village of Subiaco consists to-day of two monasteries, St. Benedict and St. Scolastica, which are under the direction of a single abbot, both a little outside the town, surrounded by the olive woods and groves, and a heap of tumbledown houses of varied architectural vintages.

As we approached I saw two monks, dressed in brown, walking in the shadow of the outer walls of the monastery. A light breeze moved the leaves of the groves around them and the bell of the convent was sounding. I went up to one and asked if it would be possible to stay the night. A fat, well-nourished man, he held the fingers of one hand in the cord around his stomach, and with the other graciously indicated the convent and the porter's lodge. We followed his instructions and found inside a group of chapels, churches, courtyards, with crowns of ivy weaving in and out of the columns. In one large square some goats and donkeys were tethered, munching peacefully, while monks and servants came and went.

We were most hospitably received by the Father Prior, who very quickly gave us permission to stay the night—somewhat to my surprise—without asking a word about my religion! (For I am not Catholic.) But it is enough apparently for these men to take one look at the face of a traveller to know whether he is Catholic, Protestant or Jew.

"We haven't had any English since the escaped prisoners in 1943," he said. "But you are as welcome as they were. We can never thank you enough for liberating us. It was *your* steadfast courage alone that saved us." And as I was shown out, he patted me on the back, as if I had been personally responsible.

It is very kind of people to do this, I know. But it has always embarrassed me on my wanderings in France and Italy—this habit of identifying me personally with our Army, Navy and Air Force. (One clerical gentleman in Nîmes in 1946, just after the war, was so delighted to see an English tourist again, that he offered me one of his few remaining bottles of Chambolle-Musigny. He would not hear of my paying for it. "I want you to look on it," he said, "as *ex voto*.")

I was now accompanied by a tall youth in lay dress to the *foresteria*. This is the name given to the part of the monastery reserved for strangers or *forestieri*. There are two classes of accommodation, depending upon the appearance of the traveller, it seems. For the most personable there is the *foresteria prima*, while the others have to be content with more modest quarters. Tramps, vagrants and beggars, after a careful scrutiny, obtain an even lower dormitory—in the stalls and outhouses. There have been several cases of thieving by such guests, I am told. But it is an unwritten law of the monastery that *no stranger* shall be turned away, however disreputable his appearance.

I was given a pleasant room, with bed-linen which appeared to have been freshly changed. The tall youth who stood beside me while I unpacked my haversack told me that I would dine in the next room at 7.30, alone; for the monks ate together in silence in their own refectory. Meanwhile, I could, if I liked, visit the chapel, where *Nunc Dimittis* had just finished. I had an hour before *Ave Maria* and vespers; and nearly two before dinner. An iron discipline evidently prevailed in all chronological matters.

I visited the chapel he spoke of, but found little of interest, except a rather embarrassing reference to the destruction of a sister institution in England by Henry VIII. The monk who acted as sacristan said that services would go on all night in this chapel, because it was a saint's day. At midnight, at three, at four and then for Mattins at six o'clock, the monks would rouse themselves and forgather for the Masses that were being said this Holy Year for the souls of all, like us, who passed on their way to Rome. *Ora pro nobis!* Twice during the night I woke to hear the monks droning these vespers and litanies, solemn, deep rhythmical voices broken only from time to time by the croaking of a raven in the gardens. And I remembered that the raven is an indispensable part of every monastery and hermitage in Italy. (It is even the emblem of the patron saint St. Benedict, whose life a raven saved. Some enemies had sent up some poisoned food to him in his hermitage, by way of variety; but before he could eat it, his pet raven had whisked it off the plate and carried it far into a forest, there depositing it safely out of harm's way!)

What interested me more than the chapel, however, was the pharmacy. I had often heard that monasteries and convents buried in the country without medical attentions, add the cares of the body to those of the soul. Certain monks become quite good herbalists and, aided by the multitude of balsamic plants growing in these wild parts, perform a sort of quack service for their colleagues and the local peasantry. The monk in charge showed me round the next morning. Among the bottles and phials I saw also skulls and relics, and even a skeleton in a case. He asked me if I required any medical attention, and I replied that my hair had a tendency to fall out.

"Ah!" he cried delightedly, pointing to his own shriven crown. "*Un calvo!*" And, taking a bottle from the shelf, he introduced me to *Aqua di Betulla*, an old peasant prescription from the bark of birch-trees. I bought a bottle and found after two months that it had an excellent effect, but at the expense of making my hairs as brittle as wires.

The young man who looked after me during my forty-eight hours in the monastery was, I discovered later, an escaped German prisoner. The Father Prior refused any payment when I left, so I gave it to this youth. I learnt that he had been in the S.S. and was still "wanted" by the Allies. I felt a little ill at ease when I reflected that I had slept under the supervision of this man—although, with his sad, attenuated features, he hardly gave the impression of being capable of any "atrocity".

But it was, I thought, worthy of the Catholic Faith that, just as these monks had harboured escaped English prisoners a few years before, so now they were doing the same thing for the other side. That universal aptness of the Roman Church, not only for all stages of civilisation, but for all sorts and conditions of men and nations, well befits her claim to divine origin. She is of all nations and all times, that wonderful Church of Rome. And here is her strength—not in the vaude-ville of her services and the politics of her Princes.

That evening before leaving, I wandered in the grounds which extend as far as the *Sacro Eremo*, where the hermit monks live. The gardens around the monastery were well tended, with boxwood hedges and lavender trees. There were fish-ponds and benches overgrown with moss and, except for an old man looking for snails at the bottom of a hedge, no life at all—for the monks were at their devotions. Near the flower-bed was a sundial, one of those complicated kinds, with several faces and apocryphal figures, to be found all over Italy; and which no foreigner can ever understand. I asked the old gardener to tell me the time from it. After pondering it for some minutes, he said gravely, "Subtract the time on the main face from 24 hours and *add* the time indicated on the secondary dial. But counted from 1 to 24 o'clock. The time thus obtained will be the hour of *Ave Maria*."

The hour of *Ave Maria*! Not some rude, arithmetical hour, of repose, or sunset—but of *Ave Maria*! I made no further Anglo-Saxon attempts on time; but waited on a bench until the sun dipped behind the oaks, the air became cool and fresh, and from the campanile, the evening bell began to toll.

The loneliness of these gardens is appropriate to an order of monks who live for most of the year as anchorites. A monk later showed me the *Sacro Eremo* where they retire. He had a fleshless, ivory face himself, like something out of an Italian painting.

"St. Benedict, our founder," he said primly, "became so disgusted with the decadence of society, that he was possessed by a *saeva indignatio*, and decided to reform the world. What remained then for such an ardent, heroic soul to do? It can be said in one word. To found a monastic order."

He then showed me some of the little one-man cottages into which they retire, where they spend weeks entirely on their own, eating, sleeping, cooking, reading, cultivating their gardens, in the intervals of pure contemplation. They live a life of complete silence. In this way, forgoing speech—(which is, after all, the key to life and intercourse)—they confine themselves as utterly as any prisoner in his cell. My German batman told me that they are allowed to address a word of greeting to their pet canary or to their flowers, arranged along the window-sills—but only in the lowest tones. Some satisfy the natural longing for human intercourse by falling in ecstasy before the statue of their favourite saint, placed by each in a niche in his cell. When they meet one another, the only greeting these silent men are allowed, as they quickly pass, is a grim *Memento Mori*!

The more I see in Italy of these men who renounce everything for such a life, the more I admire them and only wish that I could attain to such spirituality. But the world is too much with me. There is too much still to see and do before retiring. In my case it would be a confession of defeat, although in theirs it is, I know, a proclamation of victory.

"Not content with the solitary life," continued the monk, "St. Benedict wrote tracts of tremendous force

against simony and nepotism. He travelled exten-
sively, founding hermitages all over France and
Dalmatia. A highly intelligent man, of an iron will,
yet with the kindest of natures and with a bewitching
smile. A man who knew men, and who spoke with
Emperors on equal terms. He did miracles and pro-
phecies and accepted death with great joy, in solitary
confinement, as he had lived."

The monks take it in turns to live in these cells,
leaving the cœnobitic house (where I was quartered),
for their isolation in the *Sacro Eremo*. Even when they
are living in the main building however, the rules
are strict. Fasting on Wednesdays and Fridays and
Saints' Days; the rule of silence. And above all,
the rule of *work*. For each monk must carry out his
allotted task—carpenter, printer, cook, bookbinder,
gardener. The life in the monastery is, they say, "the
life of Martha, that is the life of Activity"; while the
other, in the *Sacro Eremo*, is "the life of Mary, of
contemplation".

The founder of this monastery, Benedict, was born in
A.D. 480. He came to Rome as a promising young man
interested in the Catholic Church, but soon forsook
the Latin city which, in spite of that least barbarian
of barbarian Emperors, Theodoric, was about to complete its contribution to civilisation. Instead, he
took to the hills here in Subiaco, where he lived in a
cave, absorbed in ecstatic visions. (The place was then
called *Sub lacus*, owing to a lake in the vicinity.) His
sister, with the odd-sounding name of Scolastica, also
retreated to this wilderness, where she seems to have
had a great influence on him. One day she persuaded him to leave his cave, and pronounce to the
world his views about Christianity—which were of a
somewhat Calvinistic kind. He did so and, to his
surprise (for monasticism was then unknown), found a

number of young Romans equally disgusted with the
frivolous decay of their city, who wished to become his
disciples. At that moment monasticism, in the form
of the Benedictine Order, was born.

When the movement at Subiaco was flourishing and
converts were appearing daily, a jealous and ambitious
rival hermit from nearby Vicovaro, called Pelasgius,
tried to discredit it. He had the effrontery to introduce
a number of beautiful young girls into the monks'
quarters. Benedict, when he realised that his monks had
behaved improperly with them, immediately forsook
the profaned place, where he had meditated and prayed
for so long in the company of three blackbirds. He
migrated to Monte Cassino, about forty miles to the
south, where he founded the famous monastery which
the English, Germans, Americans and Poles recently
destroyed, and which throughout the barbarism of the
Dark Ages kept civilisation alive, the monks indus-
triously copying, writing, annotating in their cells—the
"lighthouse of learning".

But to return to Subiaco. During the Gothic period
it did not prosper. The Lombards sacked it in A.D. 601,
and the monks took refuge in Rome when their
monastery was nothing but a bit of rock again. It was
at this, the second difficult moment of its history, that
Gregory the Great really gave the Benedictine Order
the power which was later to become worldwide.

Like the Donation of Constantine to the Papacy,
there is an apocryphal document, a *parchment*, in which
Gregory is supposed to have granted the Benedictines
a number of rights over the souls of human beings
(a considerable concession in those days). On this their
pretensions have been based ever since. The only
version of this document we have to-day is a copy,
describing itself as authentic, of A.D. 1654. But as the
period of time between the alleged donation and the
copy is greater than that between William the Conqueror

and George VI of England, there is reason to doubt its authenticity. A number of similar "donations" to the order appeared later—notably those of Gregory IV and Nicholas I, and of the Bohemian Kings, Hugues and Lothaire—but the apocryphal copies and elaborations of these were so considerable that Pope Leo IX burnt them all with his own hands in A.D. 1051.

The Abbey spent nearly two centuries during the Lombard period without life, a heap of blackened ruins on a mound. In A.D. 760, Pope John VII rebuilt and populated it again with monks. The Saracens destroyed it entirely in A.D. 840 and killed all the monks. Pope Peter I rebuilt it in A.D. 880. The Hungarians knocked it down again in A.D. 938; and Pope Benedict VII erected it again in 981. Since then it has, except for the depredations of time and earthquakes and odd cannon balls that have lodged in its walls, not only remained intact, but has flourished—in the purely temporal sense of that word.

Historians like Gregorovius say that its power dates from this moment when it became so rich that even local barons gave it towns and castles to ingratiate themselves with the Abbot. The Abbots became barons themselves, and from this moment their monastery seems to have escaped from religious control altogether. The first purely temporal Abbot was John V, a powerful and warlike man who, for fifty-three years, reigned here as absolutely as a king, with a paid army, riding off to war with sword at side and shield in hand, against the neighbouring feudal potentates. The Church militant!

He enriched the monastery with their possessions, before dying full of years in 1121. He is, one might say, the Julius II of the Benedictine Order. After this the Abbots of Subiaco became redoubtable Campagna princes, like the Orsinis or the Colonnas, with whom they were frequently at war. Their vassals, the serfs and peasants of their fiefs, groaned beneath a feudal despotism all the more fearful because it was exercised in the name of Christ. To the temporal power of life and death belonging to the ordinary lord was added the more terrible one of eternal damnation.

Nor were the monks who operated under their Abbot liege less bellicose. In 1276, after the death of an Abbot, one of them, Pelagus, decided to have done with this hypocrisy. He accordingly proclaimed himself Baron and Temporal Lord of Subiaco. He attacked the cloisters with his soldiers, chased out any monks who opposed his idea, took possession of the treasure and retired to an impregnable castle in the vicinity, where he lived surrounded by warriors and women until the Pope in Rome (who had put up with a good many abuses at Subiaco) was at last obliged to send an army and rout him out. A long and difficult siege was necessary before this belligerent monk was defeated.

The effect of the Papal exile at Avignon was even more regrettable. His Holiness, from the banks of the Rhone, sent a friend of his, Bartholomew of Monte Cassino, as Abbot. This man established a brothel in the monastery and enlisted only monks interested in it. The fate that overtook them however, was more than a punishment for their sins. For on his death, a violent ascetic, François Adhemar, replaced him as Abbot, and hanged seven of these monks upside down over a slow fire.

Things reached a climax when fifteen young men of the town amused themselves by making long noses at his monks, and setting their dogs on them in the street. The monks complained to the Abbot. The next night, this ferocious disciplinarian sent his soldiers to arrest the young men, all of whom belonged to the best families of Subiaco. At dawn the next day, the inhabitants were horrified to see them hanging from gibbets erected on a place which, even now, is known as "the hill of the gibbet". This was too much for the population. They rose, attacked the monastery, set fire to it, killed the monks and threw the Abbot out of the window.

It was at this point that Pope Urban VI decided to take matters in hand by henceforth nominating the Abbot himself (hitherto the election had been left largely to the monks). The first Abbot under this new system was Juan Torquemada, and his successor was Roderigo Borgia, who later became Pope Alexander VI. And yet both these men—whose names still send a shudder through good Christians—were accounted, by previous Subiaco standards, reasonable, mild and tractable.

The Colonna family obtained possession of the Abbey in 1508 and reigned there for 116 years without any pretence at apostolic succession, because, at this moment, the Papacy had reasons for placating this powerful Campagna dynasty. The Pope granted them the right of transferring the post of Abbot to the Abbot's nephew, Colonna nephew replacing Colonna nephew as Abbot.

The wealth of Subiaco became so great that it was worth a major war to obtain suzerainty over it. And during this time the family was continually at war— even with the Pope himself! On June 27th, 1527, the Papal armies were utterly routed outside Subiaco and their flag hung in the church as a trophy, where every year since, on the same date, a procession before it celebrates the great victory of the Colonna over the Vicar of Christ.

As one would expect, the Colonna's reign at Subiaco was a feudal one, even though it took place after the Renaissance. But that family, the oldest in Italy, has always distinguished itself more in the arts of war than in those of peace; and they kept the tradition up nobly. The monks became train-band captains, levying war right and left in the Campagna. In 1500 the terrible Cenci matricide took place at Subiaco, about which Shelley wrote his play. The last Cardinal-Abbot of the Colonna house lived here quite openly with his mistress, Arthemise, who replaced him in charge of the Abbey whenever he was called away.

It was at the beginning of modern times that the more recent families, the Borghese and Barberini, appeared at Subiaco and, supported by the nepotism of the Popes, began to dispute possession. From now on, the power of the Colonna family declines. The pictures on the walls of the Convent of St. Scolastica tell the story. The rude barons in cuirasses and chain-mail change into effeminate princes in embroidered waistcoats and silk stockings. This is the new Spanish epoque of gallant sensuality. A Borghese obtained the post of Abbot in 1608, but he was chased out by the Barberini in 1633, who kept the power in their hands, as the Colonna had, for the next 100 years. What the Colonna had done in their armour, the Borghese and Barberini now did in their buckled shoes and powdered perruques. For their authority was no less absolute than that of the ruder barons, and they meted out the same justice—to the terror of the inhabitants. So severe were their laws that for merely having poached a pheasant a man was sentenced to ten years in the galleys.

The last scene of all in this sad Christian story took place in the middle of the eighteenth century, when the people, exasperated beyond belief by their sufferings, started the final revolution against the Abbot and his monks. They sang songs ridiculing them, and read aloud in the streets the story of the violence and oppression of the last 1,000 years. The Barberini Abbot attempted the old high-handed methods of his predecessors. But it was the age of Voltaire—even in Italy. A rising took place and the good offices of the Pope were requested by both parties. Benedict XVI, to his eternal credit, had the courage to take the part of the people against the monks of his patron saint. And in 1753 he abolished for ever the temporal power of the Cardinal-Abbot of Subiaco.

Thus, after over 1,000 years, a Benedict put an end to what a Benedict had begun. Only a few formal titles were left to the monks. The whole temporal power and its revenues passed to the Papal State. In the words of an Italian historian, "from that time, the story of Subiaco loses interest".

CHAPTER NINETEEN

The English in Tivoli

IF YOU LOOK out due east across the Campagna from Rome, you will see the slopes of Tivoli in the distance—vague blue shapes situated on the edge of this wall of the Sabine mountains in which we had been travelling, little distant from Rome in mileage; of secular distance in everything else. It was only now, just before Tivoli, that I became really aware of this contrast of old and new—of the technical civilisation of the last fifty years imprinting itself, as irresistibly as any Angevine or Bourbon tyranny, on the ancient soil of Italy. A huge hoarding of silk-encased female legs outside Tivoli, and another of a fat, jolly man exhorting us to drink Cinzano Vermouth as we entered the town, spoke eloquently of 1950.

Not only man, but his machines began to change. The interminable peasants turned into *bons bourgeois*; the occasional Abruzzi imitation of a motor car turned into a smart American "automobile"; the bray of the donkey was drowned by the two-tone klaxon; and the *Vespa* motor-scooter, symbol of modern Italy (symptom of it one might say), became more ubiquitous and deafening than ever. At Tivoli our Sabine journey clearly ended.

There was an air of gentility too, about the approaches to the town, with their avenues of plane-trees, flowered cottage gardens and well-tended box hedges. One suddenly felt that there was really such a thing as a middle class in Italy; and I half expected to see English ladies in *villegiatura*, with sunshades and novels and embroidery. Like Fiesole, every hill, every view of Tivoli seemed familiar—to have been made famous by some painter or poet.

L

But there are hardly any English left in Tivoli to-day. This city, which was to the Roman English what Fiesole is to the Florentine English, has been deserted by its Lady Browns and Lady Fiona Fenwicks. Those that remain, squeezing an uncertain income out of England from their stocks and shares, know that at any moment war, famine or the Government at home may leave them stranded. Most have therefore migrated from Tivoli to surer climes—South Africa, Vancouver, Rhodesia, Kenya, the new "fortunate isles" of Horace, for which the Roman nobles also yearned when their civilisation was crumbling. A handful of Americans have replaced them.

This exodus has surprised (and pained) many of the older natives, the Marios, Pepes and Beppos who, for two centuries, have buttled and suttled obsequiously for the upper-British middle classes under the impression that they are its aristocracy. On my second day, an old waiter in the hotel said to me mournfully: "Why do you English no longer come? Have we not an English church? An English cemetery. . . ?"

I tried to explain what has happened to us since we won two wars and lost them. But the paradox was too difficult in Italian.

It is true that in the cemetery of which he spoke, or at least in a corner of it, there is a fairly eloquent tribute to the love the English have always had for this town of cascades and fountains. The number of English gentlewomen who have expired here quietly, among the mimosa and cyclamen, is considerable. Their average age must be about eighty. Among their tombs I found this inscription:

In loving memory of Major-General B. S. G. P——
Sometime Deputy and Assistant Attorney-General
and
Member of Gray's Inn. Also for many years
Recorder of the Rolls,

Who fell asleep on the 2nd June, 1872, while
On a journey in the land he loved.
"Vivitur ingenio, cætera mortis erunt."

I do not like to speak disrespectfully of the dead;
but I do think that a Major-General, and a British
one at that, should die in another way—or if he did
fall asleep, not mention it.

Looking at these tombs, surrounded by those of
Germans, French, Scandinavians, Russians, I wondered how much the Italians really distinguish us
from the other foreigners who have laid their bones in
their pleasure resorts. I suspect that we English are
looked on simply as another brand of barbarian, more
hypocritical and commercial, if less musical and cruel,
than the Teuton. Is there not a maxim, *"l'Inglese più
secco di un merluzzo"* (the Englishman drier than a
codfish)? But the Italians are far too polite to say this
to our faces. And so, even to-day, we English still go
about quite happily in Italy, self-confidently, lording
it lightly, being swindled gracefully, under the impression that we are much respected. When the Italian
finally realises that we are no longer monied—and I
am surprised how long he is taking about it—then
perhaps we shall find that this respect dies much more
quickly than we would hope.

That we shall be replaced by other plutocrats in Tivoli
is certain. For this city has always been, from earliest
times, a place for the rich—the Roman emperors, the
Renaissance Popes and Princes, the Anglo-Saxon nabobs
of the Steel Age: they have all trooped here from Rome
in the hot season, to indulge their whims and wants and
vices. Why should the Atomic Age be any different?

The Roman Emperor Hadrian, on retiring to his villa
outside Tivoli here in A.D. 134, caused a host of elaborate
buildings to be erected, in imitation of the great
edifices he had seen on his tour round the world—the

Lyceum, the Pokile of Athens, the Canopus of the Nile, an exact imitation of the Vale of Tempe in Thessaly, even Tartarus the underworld, as described by the poets.

The Renaissance Prince, Ippolito d'Este, indulged his tastes in the same way 1,500 years later at the Villa d'Este, by getting his architect, Ligorio, to harness the River Anio and run it through the garden, where it reissued in the form of 1,000 fountains. One of these, inspired perhaps by his predecessor's building mania, is called the *Rometta*, or little Rome, an exact reproduction of the buildings of ancient Rome, each with its watery jet. Another consists of a number of bronze birds, perched on hollow pipes shaped like the branches of a Judas-tree, which sing and whistle under the action of the water flowing at high pressure; the singing ceases abruptly with the appearance of a mechanical owl in the tree, the silence then being broken at intervals by the screeches of the night-bird. In the true Tivoli tradition, this Prince was also a music-lover. Perhaps the most charming fountain of all was a hydraulic organ, which played day and night.

Music, as much as ornamental architecture, is I found, the symbol of Tivoli. In these gardens, where Palestrina walked and composed; and where 300 years later Liszt, the guest of the family, wrote those most exquisite of programme pieces, *I Cipressi di Villa d'Este* and *Le Fontane di Villa d'Este*, music is still to be heard. The popular outdoor opera of the sixteenth century is still alive in the squares and piazzas of Tivoli.

It was in such a piazza that I found myself a few nights later. A stage had been erected, with a *papier-mâché* pediment on which, true to the millenary tradition, was crudely depicted a drunken Silenus in the midst of a troupe of frolicking satyrs and fauns. Here, before an audience drawn from all classes of the community, the singers made up for any little vocal failings by sheer animal good spirits. Surrounded by the buzz of continual conversation, I found the true musicality of the Italian race, punctuated by the drawing of corks. *Otello*, most Italian of operas, was here appreciated as much as it has ever been by the pundits of Covent Garden and the Metropolitan.

Unlike so many operas, where the action is over-dramatised to the point of farce, it is perfectly wedded to the music in *Otello*. Although it is a story everyone knows by heart, time and again I felt a great throb go through the audience, as they were moved by the passion of Otello, or appalled by the blandishments and devilries of Iago. The singer of Desdemona, a plump, good-natured Sicilian, gave everything that her lungs contained, and received ovations worthy of Patti. In these three characters Verdi is surely the great Italian master, depicting perfectly the nature of his people. They are the masterpieces of his art. Here Desdemona is the eternal woman placed beside the two Italianate men, simply as an excuse for them to get passionate, crafty, violent and jealous, in fact, Italian. Here, that beloved theme, of jealousy culminating in sudden death, is perfectly adapted to the hand of the musician; and opera is, as it should be—based upon the emotions aroused by the human voice, not in the richness of the accompaniment or other instrumental felicities.

I went to this opera with an Englishman I had met in the hotel, one of our rare survivals, wintering in Tivoli on some dollars he had earned in America. He was a journalist and had a special "pass" to visit the singers behind in their boxes during the interval, on which he kindly offered to take me.

It was extraordinary to see the power of the word "journalist" on these struggling singers. Otello was in his little tent, busy putting on more black; but when he heard we had arrived he rushed out and drew us in, and began producing photographs of himself.

"American journalist?" he said to me excitedly.

I explained that I was not a journalist. But my English friend immediately began to take notes about him—for no other reason, I think, than to quieten him. I was listening admiringly to the technical skill of the journalist being receptive when I was suddenly whisked off by a sort of major-domo in a uniform to interview Cassio, in another tent. Before I had time to deny again that I was a journalist, Cassio had started vouchsafing information about himself.

"I was born," he said breathlessly, "at Suraccia, a village near Capua. You wouldn't know it, of course. But you could say it was near Pietranera, where Gigli came from. You should also add that it has its own opera—a village affair, you understand. And it was here that, at the age of nine, I first sang. In the *castrato* role, of course. But it was at the San Carlo, Naples, that I really made my début. Here too my grandfather used to sing. A bass-baritone, Mario Colao, something of a local celebrity. I shall probably visit the States next year. . . ."

I got out a notebook and began taking all this down.

"What paper will it be in?" he said immediately.

I explained that I wrote for a group of papers and couldn't promise definitely (determining to give all the information to the journalist). This only made him all the more informative, because he thought it would be in more than one paper. He reminded me of those travellers you meet in American trains, who tell you their life history before you have even introduced yourself. When I left, he gave me a signed photograph of himself as Don Ottavio.

I noticed that his cubicle, like that of all the singers, had on its table a little collection of personal photographs, not only of *Babbo* and *Mamma*, but also, in *every case*, of the Madonna, either a coloured postcard

or a statuette. This is an affair of life or death for these
people, I could well understand. I hope that Cassio's
Madonna overheard our conversation that evening.

When we returned to the theatre for the second act,
a small transformation had taken place in the seats
around us. Near us during the first act, had sat a
family consisting of the biggest father, mother and
two daughters I have ever seen, all of approximately
the same size. They had reserved four seats, but were
easily occupying five. And as the ticket-holder of the
fifth had not yet come, it looked as though we should
be reasonably comfortable for the rest of the evening.
Unfortunately, during the interval, he had arrived.
A difficult situation now arose, of which we were the
witnesses. It was clearly impossible for the family to
get into their four seats; equally clearly the newcomer
wanted the fifth. At last, one of the daughters, after
attempting vainly to pour a quart into a pint pot, got
up and, without the slightest show of ill-grace at this
confession of volume, offered to go. "I will find Uncle
Giacomo," she said, laughing.

I saw her at the next interval, sitting happily
perched up at the back, on a *gradinata*, with an equally
big man, bulging good-naturedly over on to their
neighbours, eating grapes.

Around us sat the opera-going public of Italy, a
most varied assortment, including even a quantity of
those urchins, who sell cigar-ends. The noise, even
during the singing, was terrific; a thousand feet and
hands seemed to be in perpetual movement, clapping,
eating, walking about, pushing, jostling, so that more
than once I felt to see if my wallet was still on me.

A characteristic feature of the open-air opera is the
absence of a curtain. All that happens is that the
arc-lamps which face the singers are reversed during
the interval and turned towards the audience—in
theory, to dazzle them while the scene is being shifted.

But this does not prevent their seeing the actors strolling about on the stage; Otello smoking a cigarette, Desdemona looking in a mirror, Iago adjusting his wig.

And then there is the open-air scenery. For this opera, elaborate walls of a mediæval castle had been erected, with crenellations, portcullises, gratings, battlements, spreading right out to both wings, where suddenly, almost as if the walls were being used for twentieth-century purposes, they turned into huge advertisements for Coca-Cola, remedies for varicose veins, talcum powder and other patent things—all as high as the battlements themselves.

That the opera was by no means the only entertainment this evening was clear in the piazza outside, where itinerant performers, hucksters, and vendors did their tricks and sold their wares by the light of little oil-lamps. And at the end the English journalist said to me, "Come into the piazza and I will show you the most beautiful thing in Tivoli!"

Wondering what he could be referring to, I went with him, and here, outside the Church surrounded by an admiring crowd, stood an elderly sword-swallower. I had watched this man once before and found little that was beautiful about him, but my new friend stopped before him. He always attracted a large crowd by his trick of stripping to the waist and replacing the sword by a long neon tube, which he swallowed down as far as the stomach—the wires coming out of his mouth to an accumulator on a chair—which was then lit up from within, so that you could see his ribs, as in an X-ray, an effect at night which was much admired.

He had just finished his turn, was sheathing his swords and tubes, and the collection was being taken by a slim, half-naked urchin. The African blood of this child was apparent in his skin and thick lips, contrasting oddly with the thin Italianate features.

"He moves," said the English journalist quietly, "with grace."

I turned and saw that he was staring at the boy, as if mesmerised. I asked him if this was the "most beautiful thing in Tivoli," and he replied that this youth had the same graceful movements, carriage and poise as a favourite nephew of his who had died quite recently, at an early age. He said that, for sentimental reasons, he would like to take him out for a meal. We approached the sword-swallower, to whom he made this suggestion. The old man was amazed that anyone should want to talk to his assistant.

"A wretch," he said, calling the boy over, "the worthless son of a worthless mother. She has sent him to plague my last hours. What he cannot rob off others, he robs off his Grandad. Look! Even now his pockets are full of what he has not handed over!"

He took hold of the boy by the ear, and with the other hand deftly ran through his pockets. They were full of 5- and 10-*lire* notes.

"Worthless!" he said, pushing him away. "He can neither read nor write. A disgrace to . . . But if your excellency wishes . . ." The English journalist was already thrusting money into his hand. . . .

The journalist now turned to the boy. "What is your favourite dish, sonny?"

The urchin had been gazing from one to the other, as if stupefied, but at this he came smartly to life. "*Ossa-buco e faggiolini, signore!*" he said.

And so it was arranged. The English journalist, musical critic of one of our most intellectual weeklies, took out "one of the most beautiful things in Tivoli" and stuffed it with *ossa-buco* and *faggiolini* in the shadow of the Rocca di Pio. . . .

I have some difficulty myself in finding much beauty in these Italian urchins perhaps, quite illogically, because I have been swindled by them so often. When one of them passes your table if you happen to be writing outside a café and lay down your pen, he has an air of such intelligence as he glances casually at you, that you feel he is saying to himself how easily he could, if he liked, steal it. At other times he will stand beside you with the air of the conventional choirboy; yet after he goes, you feel your pockets. He seems to be already twenty-five and has the cocksureness of a New York journalist. His precocity is almost legendary. At the Liberation he was money-changer, pimp and paramour all at the same time. It is easy to understand the enthusiasm of foreign artists, writers and people like my English journalist for such picturesqueness. The Italians too are now using these *monelli*—as actors in films; for two main reasons, it seems. They are cheap to film; and they satisfy the modern passion for ugliness in art.

What troubles me most about these urchins, I think, is that for all their picturesqueness, they are really a sinister parody of what a child should be. The graces, faiths and simplicities of childhood are all absent in this undernourished, unkillable little infant of the poor.

I met one other Englishman while I was in Tivoli— of a rather different type, and with whom I exchanged no word, but merely admired from a distance. It was in the *Acque Albule*, the old thermal baths of the Romans, on my last day in Tivoli. These baths lie about five miles to the west in the Campagna and announce themselves to the approaching traveller by the pungent smell of sulphuretted hydrogen. For a moment, as we neared them, I thought I would be asphyxiated, and contemplated going back; but interest in the *thermæ* where Cæsar and Augustus bathed, overcame my distaste.

With memories of Roman Bath in England I entered, expecting naumachies and columns and *pistaccio*-coloured water, with one or two elderly gentlemen sitting back perhaps in pneumatic ease on air cushions. Instead I found sunburnt youths and maidens playing water-pool in an absolutely modern swimming bath; afterwards taking a cocktail round the bar at the end.

"Come to the baths where Cæsar, Marius and Sextius Calvus bathed!" cries the brochure of the *Stabilimento Termale*. "With fifty-two cabins, a heated observation gallery, forty-one vapour douches, a room for inhaling and pulverisation. A cocktail bar! We have three radiotherapy experts. Our water contains bicarbonate and calcium! It is limpid, without colour, smell or taste. It can be drunk. It is excellent for the circulation of the blood, varicose veins, arthritis, and illnesses of the uterus, above all those complicated by neurotic effects. . . ."

These baths have, in a sense, clearly returned to the purpose of their Roman inventors. For the *thermæ* were originally Spartan in intention, to exercise the body. It was only in the later days of the Roman Empire that the baths became Asiatic and effeminate, with milk-warm water, often perfumed, and special vapour baths; often the scenes of open vice and debauchery.

The Englishman I saw here was an elderly, portly person, who sat reading a book at the side, maintaining somehow a sort of dignity in spite of wearing only a towel. We did not speak, instinctively conscious of the unwritten rule that Englishmen abroad always ignore one another. But I could not help noticing the book he was reading. It was the *Satyricon*—in the Everyman edition. And I felt truly, among these bounding youths, that he was the last representative of a departed world. For those days when every English traveller read the Latins—when Virgil was regarded as an English country gentleman and Horace had chambers in Albany, and both had been at Eton, are almost over. The English *milord* is gone or going. Or put more bluntly, the reign of pound sterling is over.

CHAPTER TWENTY

Rome

THE LAST STAGE of our journey took us past the Roman airfield of Ciampino, to the south-east of the city, surrounded by those fragments of broken Claudian aqueduct which are the most Roman things in the Campagna—a contrast of old and new, of reticulated brick and concrete runway, of aeroplane and Pepe, our donkey; now further emphasised by a vast advertising campaign on hoardings, of Pagliari perfumed ladies, Bemberg underwear and yellow tigers nourished on Shell petrol.

Not far from the tomb of the early martyr, Santa Cecilia, we stopped to examine the Claudian aqueduct. Although dilapidated and sporadically non-existent, striding across the landscape, this structure still dominates it. Such was the confidence of the builders in its power to endure, that they have even arranged little holes in the masonry for the scaffolding required at repair-time. You can still see them. I had known this aqueduct before as most people no doubt have, from the paintings of Claude Lorrain; that "ideal" background, where the Roman masonry serves as a setting for a shepherd and his flock in a field of flowers, surrounded by flimsily clad, dancing maidens. Nearby, will be some centurions looking romantically at the maidens, behind whom stands a Corinthian temple. On the left may be cascades, or perhaps the Tyrrhenian Sea with a red lateen sail upon it.

Did such a landscape ever exist? Or is it only the Petrol Age which has made it seem impossible to-day?

Past us as we jogged along to Rome tore buses and motor cars, conveying busy people to and from the Roman airport.

What was agreeable however, was that I felt no sense of incongruity on Pepe, whose 3,000 years of transport seemed well-rooted in the landscape. Nor did any of the passers-by pay the slightest heed to us, as they would have on the Great West Road or some other British equivalent, for their own modes of transport were hardly more advanced. I was pleased at one point to see a cart containing a selection of bric-à-brac, on top of which slept an old fellow with a clay pipe. In a field on the left, we passed a cow up to its neck in a bog, surrounded by vociferating peasants, but looking quite contented and placid—no doubt, because it had struck bottom. Fast American limousines swished by; but also broken-down Fiats of the twenties, coughing along, a bare improvement on Pepe. There were tramps and vendors, cyclists and housewives, chickens and geese, children and dotards. All kinds and conditions of man accompanied us as we entered the City.

Masceri had never been in Rome before, but it made small impression on him; for on my suggesting that, as I had booked a room in a *pension*, we should find something for him, where he could stable Pepe for the night before returning to Terni, he thanked me but said he would prefer to be getting back immediately.

"You intend to travel all night?" I asked.

"Yes," he said, tapping the donkey's saddle. "I can snooze on his back."

In a café not far from the bridge, we settled our finances over a glass of wine, and I thanked him for his agreeable company. Then I watched them both lumping down the road together in the direction of the Milvian Bridge and the Campagna again. Dear

Masceri, I thought as I saw him go, you have just entered the capital of your country—of, some say, the world—for the first time in your life; you have walked along one of its suburban streets, saluted it with a glass of wine—and returned home on your donkey!

It is said of Rome that it does not, like Venice or Florence, immediately ravish the newcomer. A sojourn of weeks, months even, is necessary before it begins to exercise an influence more subtle and insinuating than that of the northern cities. This purgatory I had passed through on a lightning Army visit six years before. The jumble of ugliness outside the station had appalled me then; so had the urchins who rushed for my cases, crying, "American soldier, wonna private car? Wonna nice gal?" The unevenness of the architecture; the grubby, overladen trams; the palpably inefficient dustman service—all these things had made me think that S.P.Q.R. may well mean, as certain anti-Roman Italians say, *"Sono porci quei Romani!"* (they're pigs, those Romans).

But it was not long, even in those military days, before I began to feel the beauty of this sordid and splendid city, leprous and incomparable; to appreciate that chaos of broken stone that fronts eternity in the Forum Romanum; above all, to appreciate the meaning of the word *Catholic*.

For Rome is Everyman's city. Not only all stages of civilisation, but all sorts and condition of man are here. Beside Rome, Paris seems provincial—in the sense that it is planned for an élite, artistic and intelligent. There is no place for the stupid or slow-witted in Paris you feel, just as there is no place for the poor in New York. In Rome it is not a crime to be any of these things. Wealth and self-conscious culture are to be seen, but they seem no more important than anything else, emerging out of this total lack of planning and organisa-

tion as anything might. The oldest monuments in the
world abut on Fifty Shilling Tailors. The streets have
a sameness, a lack of magnificence, a London atmosphere of grime and cheery self-confidence. Nothing
appears to have been planned for effect. Where beauty
appears, someone seems to have been at work unconsciously, for his own amusement almost. The Arch of
Constantine in the shadow of the Coliseum has not
been placed there specially—there just happened to
be room at that point; whereas in Paris, the same thing
is placed on a hill, visible for miles from all sides,
approached by twelve avenues in star formation, with
an eternal fire beneath.

There is only one self-consciously magnificent building in Rome, the Sugarloaf or Victor Emmanuel
monument on the Capitol; and only one magnificent
thoroughfare, the Via dell' Impero, laid out during
the recent nationalistic period. And both are really
products of Teutonism—that Teutonism which has
perennially mesmerised the Italian, fortunately without
ever mastering him.

There are really two Romes for me, the Rome
of my imagination and the Rome I find three days
after arriving. The first consists of nightingales on
the Aventine and sunsets on the Campagna, ilex
shadows and grey spaces in the evening in the Villa
Borghese gardens, whose terraces are adorned with
rostral columns and marble bas-reliefs, interspersed
with cypresses and pines—where the ghost of Nero is
still said to wander.

The second Rome is a place of urchins and street-
vendors and beggars; booths in Trastevere on which
every conceivable object is displayed for sale; stuffs,
pots, pans, haberdashery, carefully selected cigar-ends,
gimcrack jewellery. My clearest memories of this second
Rome are of Abyssinians in white burnouses, selling drugs
and patent medicines among the taxi-stands; of sweating,

semi-naked men in chains, surrounded by gaping mobs, announcing with lungs of bronze that for 10 *lire* from each bystander, they will escape from a tank of boiling oil. I still see an aged female at the Porta Pia, of whom I once unwisely asked the price of an orange; and who, for answer, took from her bosom, a rusty metal spike with "50 LIRE" printed on it which, without a word, she triumphantly thrust into one of them. Somehow my Roman memories are closely connected with fruit—oranges, grapes, lemons and water-melons on fly-blown stalls, served by scrofulous old women.

The Abyssinians used to stand near the Church of Santa Maria in Trastevere, as black as ebony in their flowing robes and turbans, selling their goods in the Oriental style, with long speeches, by wooing rather than advertising. I watched them frequently, but I never saw them sell anything. One day they were auctioning a British battledress, and for a quarter of an hour I watched an impassioned harangue. For here, since there is no fixed market price, the only way is to name a high figure and work persuasively down.

"This splendid uniform," cried the tall, good-looking chieftain, "is an article *di lusso*, worn by the British Army . . ." and he went on to invest the drab piece of khaki with such an aura of romance, with tales of the sand of the desert, of the 103rd Motorised Division, of *Montgoomeri* and the flying columns, that it seemed unusable, fit only for a collector's cabinet.

This tendency, to put the military flotsam and jetsam left over after the war to practical uses, is characteristic—perhaps more than anything else—of the modern, impoverished Roman. Here you will see beggars in British gas-capes; ice-cream men in Guards greatcoats (even in summer); taxi-drivers in Tank Corps berets; American jeeps on tyreless rims driving circus machinery; Army lorries as timber pantechnicons. These are only a few of the modern oddities to be found alongside the broken columns and plinths of another dead civilisation. The Italian is ingenious and, even if given a motor-bike, he will turn it into something else—as the complementary bus-service at the end of the war showed.

For this service, a fleet of ten British Army motor-bikes had been converted by some clever enterprise, each with a little wooden superstructure, containing benches to hold about six people—and a third wheel attached at the side. To go in this juggernaut cost 20 *lire*, but such was the tumult in the corporation trams that people sometimes risked it. I saw one of these machines, on being rather sharply held up at a cross-roads by a policeman in the Via Veneto, suddenly fall to pieces—a pile of nuts and bolts and irate people sprawling in the middle of the most fashionable street in Rome.

The Italian loves all forms of mechanical invention, preferring them if possible to be audible. A vacuum-cleaner, an electrical ice-cream-stirrer, an *espresso* coffee-machine —these things mean more to him if they make a good noise. To stand on the battlements of the Castello Sant' Angelo (as I did a few evenings later) is to be conscious of two things; on the one hand, the beauty of the scene, the eye ranging from the nearby gilded dome of St. Peter's across a sea of spires and towers to the distant Campidoglio and the Palatine with its cypress greenery and russet-coloured brick; and, on the other, of the devilish din beneath, as cars and bikes erupt their way across the city of the Cæsars. Add to this the hoarse cries of the vendors, the corncrake shrieks of the women selling lottery tickets, and from time to time, the passage of the *Nucleo Celere*, their klaxons blaring endlessly; and you have some idea of the Hell's Kitchen that is modern Rome.

M

The first Rome, the Rome of my imagination, came to me—as it does no doubt to most newcomers—in the Coliseum. I stood there alone one evening after dinner and found that this arena, one of the largest pieces of Antiquity in the world, is inhabited to-day mainly by lizards, rats, frogs and other forms of rodent. If you stand on one of the lower tiers when there is a moon and no one is about and look down, an extraordinary biological life will parade before you. While I was there, a shower of rain had filled up the hollows in the fallen bricks and marbles, and the rats came out to drink—huge brutes whose forefathers, scrambling over these same columns, had fed, I supposed, on the remains of gladiators and lions and Christians: classical rats with ancestral tails and vestigial habits. I threw a brick down, but they went on eating.

It would be interesting to know what is their normal diet. Under one arcade, near a broken column, lay a dead cat, half consumed. No doubt these rats, in their ceaseless war with the hereditary enemy, eat as much as they are eaten. An arena cat must be as tasty a morsel as one can expect—enough at any rate to annoy the arena beggar when they eat it; for he regards all refuse here as his by right.

These beggars, like the moneychangers in the Piazza Colonna, form a select guild or trades union. Rightly regarding the Coliseum as the first "beat", for which every tourist makes on arrival, they do not suffer rivals gladly, human or animal. And one morning I saw them actually turning away another, unaffiliated beggar who had hastily hobbled up when an American limousine arrived. Here, where the Cæsars once entered in state, only a small, hand-picked group of men may importune.

There is a Papal tradition dating, I believe, from the consecration of the Coliseum, when the first Cross

was erected, that because so much Christian blood
had been spilt in it, no living thing should ever be
put to death here again. But the beggar pays little
heed to this pious injunction. I saw one of them
the next day standing behind a pillar, holding a
long bit of wooden board with a nail in it, waiting
to kill a rat which was inspecting some rubbish on the
other side. But when he struck, the animal was too
quick and darted away. It is axiomatic that time, like
evolution, always helps the hunted; and this struggle,
of rat, cat and beggar, has been going on too long
now for the beggar to win. His only prey is the
tourist. In this arena, history with its blood and tears
becomes æsthetics for the tourist and economics for
the native.

A number of sculptured phalluses still stick out
above you in the vaults of the amphitheatre. They
seem to have escaped the attentions of the puritanical
bishops of the last century, who had most of them
removed and placed in the museums. The origin of
their meaning here is uncertain. A theory that these
phalluses are connected with the bull and that bull-
fights took place here as long ago as the first century
is advanced by some people. Others, however, explain
it as flattery to the memory of the deified Augustus.
This Prince, according to Suetonius, was born in a
house decorated with a frieze of erotic bulls.

What sort of spectacles did one see here? Historians
tell of lions and tigers, but the wall of the *podium* is
only 6 feet high, and they would have been a danger
to the spectators. There are no reports, however, of
anyone being killed by the beasts (except of course
the criminals and Christians). I am told they have
recently dug up ivory cylinders which revolved on
axles, and are supposed to have lined the top walls
of the *podium*; these would have prevented the animals
from crawling up. But it seems more probable that

M*

the animals were chained or caged and the victims thrown to them.

Normally in Italy I always take a guide. Whatever he says, true or untrue, is bound to be picturesque. And that morning, in the Coliseum, I joined a conducted group under a man who assured us that he knew more about the Coliseum than any other guide in Rome—admitting at the same time that the subject was so vast that there were inevitably certain gaps, even in *his* knowledge. Confronted with such modesty (unusual in an Italian), I began to think that he really might know something about it. He had one or two good anecdotes, it is true; but he treated it all rather like a university professor, giving a recital of the martyrs under Diocletian as if it were a catechism. He had been Germanised. "Sometimes during the war," he boasted, "I had to show around as many as five hundred German soldiers a day." *Sehenswürdigkeiten!*

We saw the interesting spectacle, at one point, of this man disputing with a beggar, who had somehow found his way on to the heights where we stood and was importuning one of our group. The guide, who was expatiating to us grandly in foreign tongues, suddenly turned on him like a cat—and out of his mouth issued a stream of dialect, which was lost on me, but which, judging by their expressions, must have been of vitriolic force. It lasted barely three seconds, but the beggar scuttled unceremoniously off, while the guide returned to his pidgin French and English again.

CHAPTER TWENTY-ONE

Modern Romans

THE WORD *PENSION* sounds ominous to English ears. It throws up visions of sad women sitting separately at little tables in a dining-room, staring fiercely at nothing, with saucers of jealously guarded butter and jam before them, which they seize up and bear away at the end. My *pension* in Rome had little of this about it, however—perhaps because it was Holy Year and all the nationalities of the world were pullulating here just how. It had two Arabs and a Persian; a Russian duchess; an Armenian meat-canner and an Australian stock-broker. There was also an American film-star unable to find a room in more luxurious quarters (for all the hotels were full). She had sixteen hat-boxes. The commissionaire told me proudly that they had weighed her luggage on her arrival. It had weighed exactly 1 ton.

This woman had a friend called Fisch—who described himself as an authentic Roman—and who one day did something I had believed to happen only in novels about Chicago. I was sitting in the *salotto* before dinner when he came in with a man, and opened an attaché case which was literally *stuffed* with currency—bank-notes, in wads of almost every known denomination—francs, pounds, dollars, belgas, pesetas, marks, even roubles: they all tumbled out and he ticked them off on a long list.

This man lived on champagne in the *pension*, an authentic member of that international finance aristocracy whose life is spent in moving from the Metropole

in Paris to the Metropole in Brussels, from Geneva to
Madrid, from Rome to New York, from Amsterdam
to London—and always with little attaché cases being
emptied in *salotti*. I got to know him a little and he
told me he was a diamond merchant. He also had an
insatiable appetite for women.

"On my last visit to Monaco, do you know," he said
gleefully, "I was sitting quite peacefully on the quay
drinking one morning, when who should sail into the
harbour in his private yacht but my old friend Alvarez,
the Portuguese sardine king! He had ten girls on board,
a swimming-pool and forty-five hands. He bought
two diamonds off me for his favourite girl and then
sailed away. Ah!"—he looked at me archly—"but not
before I had been on board and had the favourite!"

If it is true that a man writes his life on his face,
that the big thinker is well-developed at the top and
the big eater at the bottom of the face, then Fisch
might be taken as an excellent example. Those good,
red chateaubriands, the burgundy and the claret, the
champagnes, had, without any roundabout journey
through the stomach it seemed, slipped straight into
his cheeks. When he ate, his whole body seemed to
bear upon the plate before him, so that even the
draughts of wine were co-ordinated, geared as it
were, to the primary movements of knife and fork.
As the waiter passed he would ask, without looking up,
for the mustard or the hot sauce. He had a racing car
in which he used to take girls down to Capri after
evening parties. He told me that he always had the
name of each girl printed on his braces the morning
after he had had her.

This man was extremely helpful to me—for changing
money. For by now, after nearly three months abroad,
I was financially in a pretty poor way, barely able to
afford the *pension* fare. And Fisch gave me the names
of certain money-changers who congregated every day

in the Piazza Colonna, whom he described as "scrupu-
lously honest". Here one morning, with my little
bundle of notes, I went.

I found his friends fixing tariffs, accosting Americans
and tourists, and boycotting rivals who were offering
lower prices and spoiling the market. They immediately took me for an American and descended on me
with the war-cry, "*Dollari! Franchi svizzeri! Changey
money?*"

"Yes," I said, first mentioning the name of Fisch,
"but I want nineteen hundred, as I see the Finance
Minister is at last leaving for Washington and the
British loan is through."

"The Minister, *signore!* Leaving for Washington,
signore! Never, *signore!* That man will never leave,
depend upon it! Not even for Scotland, *signore!*
Sterling will drop from this very moment, you will
see."

He then gave me a host of reasons why the Italian
Government was about to change, had in fact already
started changing, this very morning—was in that state
known in England as anarchy and here as democracy,
when the currency fluctuates from day to day, hour to
hour, when no one does any work for weeks, because
the only sane activity for a man is speculation. He
assured me that in the turmoil that was about to start
the *lire* would mount gloriously, because the "traitors"
in the Government were about to be chased away and
put in prison. It was worth my while to buy *lire*
immediately.

"Nineteen hundred," I said.

"Seventeen fifty," he replied.

"Nineteen hundred."

"Seventeen seventy-five."

"Nineteen hundred."

We went on like this for some time, until an agree-
ment was reached—at 1,810. He then asked me to

step aside to a nearby café out of the way of the police, among other money-changers and their clients—whom I found examining notes, questioning watermarks, consulting apocryphal bank-lists. And a quarter of an hour later, bulging with those vast wads of 1,000-*lire* notes as big as flannels, which he gave me in return for the crisp little notes I had brought from the efficient north, I staggered off to thank Fisch in the *pension*.

Fisch asked me, with professional pride, how my bargaining had gone. I told him the price I had paid and he checked for me. I was amazed at the speed with which he did calculations in his head. He could in a trice multiply 34 by 1,850, and he seemed to be able to turn pounds, shillings and pence into *lire* almost without thinking. (The word the Italians use for such a man, I have since found, is the onomatopoeic *vispo*.)

Among the girls Fisch dined with at the *pension* was, as I have said, the American film-star with the ton of luggage and the hat-boxes. He seemed to have some hold on this luscious woman, who, one would have imagined, could have easily had some more palatable, if less affluent, lover. But no doubt a bottle of champagne a night was sufficient to hold her. She was working in the film on the life of St. Paul, *Quo Vadis*, being made in Rome at this moment. I never discovered what was her role in this, and it gave me a good deal of pleasure to conjecture what it might be.

Both she and Fisch were extremely kind to me, for, hearing that I was interested in art, they invited me one evening to a party in the *palazzo* of an American millionairess friend of theirs, who was much connected with art and artists; where most of the "artists" acting in the film *Quo Vadis* were to be found.

"Come and meet Betty Banker-Downs!" they cried.

And the film-star added: "She is the new Mæcenas of Rome."

At the time I knew nothing about the film or Betty Banker-Downs and, thinking that the new Mæcenas of Rome might well be the new Pierpont Morgan of Rome—with a fair selection of Old Masters about to be packed and shipped to the west—I gladly accepted. I was not quite prepared, however, for what I found.

At 6.30 the next evening, I found myself in a large, palatial building near the Pincio, surrounded by a quantity of young men, dressed in a variety of clothes from togas to tuxedos, all drinking dry Martinis and talking English. In one corner was an oil painting covering an entire wall, of a whale in a feather-bed. In another was a machine in which you put a ping-pong ball at the top in a hole, and then, laughing uproariously, watched it roll down to the bottom while it rang a series of bells on the way. There were also a number of very modern sculptures. Fisch introduced me to a young man who was the son of our hostess, with round gazelle-like eyes and spectacles, like Harold Lloyd. I was informed that this brilliant youth, although only twenty-one, had just finished his sixth novel. I asked him what it was about, and he gazed at me abstractedly through the tortoiseshell frames for some time.

"Lesbians, of course," he replied at length.

"You . . . er . . . know . . . about them?" I said, somewhat taken aback.

"Of course," he said, as if it were the most normal thing in the world. "My mother is one."

His mother was a bird-like, little, pretty person, with a retroussé nose and dark, vivacious eyes. After she had shown us all her exhibits, she turned sadly, almost with tears in those eyes, and said how awful it was to think of another war, and that all these beautiful things might be destroyed.

"What is it that Shelley says?" she sighed.

"Cease! Must Hate and Death return?
Cease! Must men kill and die?"

The answer to this question is, "Yes", and I felt like telling her to go to Subiaco.

The ornamental grounds of her fifteenth-century garden were enriched this evening by her famous, personal collection, flown at her own expense from New York, of the stone and steel art of the twentieth century, now disposed and illuminated among the myrtle bushes and parterres of roses. She had invited half the aristocracy of Rome, impoverished persons for the most part who were to be found at a turn of the garden before some piece of modern work, in search of a suitable epithet, displaying informed curiosity and yet, at the same time, a restraint proper to their station: "significant", "sensitive", "nervous" were the terms most frequently employed.

One of the most admired exhibits was a large granite naked woman, recumbent, which had recently won an important prize in Venice. Of this our hostess said to a group of admirers on whose outskirts I stood: ". . . The secret of Bill North's success lies surely in his immense respect for his material. It is through this appreciation of the essential character of stone, that he has developed his half-woman, half-landscape idiom. Surely this represents a tremendous nature poetry of a new kind. . . ."

Somewhat baffled, I afterwards asked one of the artists what it means exactly for a sculptor "to have a respect for his material." This consists largely, it appears, in leaving it alone. You find a block in a quarry looking like a sleeping woman; you transport it and then try to leave it as much as possible as it is, and not knock it about as Phidias or Michelangelo did.

Another much-admired section of her exhibits was the one devoted to sponges. These had been specially

procured for her over a three-year period in the
Venetian lagoons, by a group of divers she had hired
and supported during this time. These sponges had
interesting, often arresting shapes; sometimes even a
trifle obscene. For it was her contention that every
human and physical action can be portrayed plastically
at some stage in the evolution of the sponge. She said
that young, struggling artists should be inspired by
these examples of submarine nature at work; and that
they would then one day belly forth great new, hitherto
undreamt-of shapes and forms and textures. . . .

What a contrast it was after all this to come out
through the great portals of her *palazzo* after midnight
and find at the gate a group of beggars, cringing, holding out their hands! "The last who shall one day be
first!" They stood there in their rags, clearly unaware
of their wonderful future, lost in admiration and envy
for those who shall one day be last, as they left the
party.

Nothing throws a more lurid light on the economic
conditions of this land. And yet, as an Italian said to
me, "It has always been so. It will never change.
Socialism will never work."

Perhaps he is right—for Italy. The impression one
obtains of this land from the earliest times, in writers
like Martial and Juvenal, is of a society divided like
this, between a small class of immensely wealthy people,
and an almost starving proletariat. A.D. 1950 is no
different from A.D. 50.

CHAPTER TWENTY-TWO

Holy Year

HOLY YEAR WAS started as an institution in 1300, and to visit Rome as a pilgrim during it has always allowed a remission of sins, if certain penances are undergone there. For each sin carries with it the need for the believer to submit to temporal punishment (the eternal one being arranged elsewhere), which, if it is not expiated during his lifetime, must be expiated in Purgatory. It is at this point that the Papal indulgence enters. By suitable acts of contrition—for instance, visiting the four great basilicas during Holy Year—the sinner may avoid the temporal punishment, and the period in Purgatory as well. This principle of the remission of sins is derived from St. Paul, who says: "The burdens of the weak shall be carried by the strong." And it is the Church herself, enriched by the lives of all her saints, who offers to bear the sins of these members. But we are here on the threshold of theological grounds which it would be wiser not to enter.

It is enough to record that Boniface VIII in 1300 regulated a system which had become somewhat disorganised all over Italy, as a result of mendicant monks and friars who demanded money from the passing pilgrims for their own buildings, orders and persons. A shrewd Churchman, this Pope realised that the new national monarchies were everywhere undermining the power of the Church, and that something must be established to counter them. Hence Holy Year—to take place at the beginning of each century.

The claim of Rome then to hold all Europe in fee may seem exorbitant to us to-day. But it must be remembered that no one then questioned his spiritual allegiance to Rome; and many gave her their temporal allegiance as well. Boniface calculated that the Church could best keep in touch with her more distant members, often overawed and dominated by their local kings, by the pilgrims who were, in fact, excellent, self-appointed, unsalaried ambassadors—whom no temporal monarch could enlist.

He accordingly announced the absolute remission of temporal punishment to all who visited the four basilicas of Rome once a day for fifteen days on foot, during Holy Year. In our time this drastic discipline (it involved walking nearly seven miles a day) has been modified. And the modern pilgrim has simply to visit each of the four—St. Peter's, St. John's, St. Paul's and St. Mary's—*once* during his stay in the city. If he can do it on foot, so much the better; but this is left to his own discretion.

Even to-day, I learned, the habit of coming on foot, not just to the Roman basilicas, but from one's home, is not dead. On June 15th, 1950, five men and women set out on the 1,800-mile walk to Rome—from London. They used forty pairs of shoes and 300 pairs of socks on the way.

My personal introduction to Holy Year came three days after my arrival in Rome, when I visited the office of the *Propaganda della Fede* in the Piazza di Spagna, where tickets are issued for Papal audiences. The waiting-room was full of people, all hoping to see the Cardinal's secretary. I heard the usher announce, as one of them went in, "The Marquis di Cibita Alvapueblos", or some such resounding title. This man, who had been sitting near me, his hat and cane draped elegantly over his knees, had stiffened uneasily a few moments before, when a dirty, tramp-like fellow had planked himself down beside us.

Some of my fellow-pilgrims were certainly drawn from the lowest rungs of society, men and women by whom one half-expected at any moment to be importuned, whose general insalubrity and odour contrasted strangely with this magnificent waiting-room, the gilded marquetry tables and Gobelin tapestries—one of which represented the gorgeous Louis XIV in audience with the equally gorgeous Papal Nuncio. But the contrast seemed less strange when I remembered that I had here to do with the *Catholic* faith.

While waiting, I looked in a side-room at the famous *Mappa Mondo* of the *Propaganda della Fede*, which describes the world at that moment when Alexander VI, the Borgia Pope, in that wonderfully arbitrary way they had in those days, divided the world between Spain and Portugal. He drew a line, a parallel of longitude somewhere off the Azores, in thick black ink. "All land discovered to the west of this line," he pronounced, "shall be Spain. All land east of it, Portugal!"

No one had thought of England in those days.

I was recalled from this examination by the voice of the usher who pronounced my name in the Italian style. I followed him into a large, circular chamber in which sat the Cardinal's secretary. He was dressed in a black cassock and silken skull cap, and on his finger glittered a superb amethyst which almost dazzled me. He had a parchment skin which gave his face an Egyptian rather than Italian wisdom, and was most courteous and suave.

"An Englishman!" he said, on hearing my request. "Ah, we do all we can for Englishmen." (I could not help feeling that he said this for every nation. But then I thought, could he, a member of a *Catholic* Church, say anything else?)

"So you are anxious to have an audience with the Holy Father?"

I said I was most anxious.

"It may be difficult to arrange a *private* audience just now, but you can probably attend at a general one. Perhaps at a *baciamano*. What is your religious denomination?"

"Church of England."

I said these words without thinking. But then suddenly, for the first time, they sounded quite heretical! Yet he wrote them down deliberately, significant, terrible they seemed, words that would once, before such a man, have consigned me in a trice to the *auto-da-fé*. He wrote them down as if they were my Christian names. (Had I said, "Communist", what would he have done?)

"Do you," he continued, "it is a pure formality—but do you know any Catholic priests or cardinals in England?"

I told him of a certain Father I had known, who had once offered me a glass of port in his college rooms. This seemed to please him, for he looked up and smiled wanly. "An excellent man!" he said.

He told me that arrangements would be made and that if I wished to be present at a service that "would interest a man of my faith", he recommended the Service of the Epiphany next Sunday in the Church of Santa Maria in Trastevere, where his Cardinal was presiding. I thanked him and took my leave.

I had particularly asked for this audience with the Pope, because there was so much talk of the next one, who, everyone said, would be American. And I wanted to see my last Italian Pope; for I feared that there might be no more of that nationality in the Atomic Age. (During the Avignon captivity, all the Popes were French.) Moreover, the present Pope himself was said to favour the election of a certain American Cardinal to the Chair of St. Peter when he died—on political grounds, it was whispered! It was for this reason that his critics called him a *papa politico*.

The American Cardinal who would replace him had been recently in Rome, where he had apparently not advanced his cause or popularity with the Romans. The manageress of my *pension* spoke slightingly of him that evening when I told her of my interview with the Cardinal's secretary. "I cannot understand," she said, "how anyone could *dream* of an American Pope! Why, do you know what that American Cardinal did when he was here? *He played tennis on the roof of the Excelsior Hotel!!*"

And this was not all. She said that he had even been seen to stop his motor car in the streets and salute friends familiarly, saying, "Hi-ya!"; and sometimes even getting out, to nose about before the shop windows!! Conduct which went down well enough in New York, no doubt. But here, in the city of St. Peter! People criticised the present Pope for being a *papa politico*, she said. It would never do to have a *papa sportivo*!

Three days later, on my last Sunday in Rome, I went to the Church of Santa Maria in Trastevere to see the Cardinal at the Service of the Epiphany, one of the most important in the Catholic Church, when the Three Wise Men bring their gifts to the Divine Infant.

Devotions in every church in Rome had been continuous since dawn; and I saw a blaze of silver and jewels and brocades before the flames of candles flickering in burnished holders on an altar, in whose niche stood a rose-wood idol, garlanded and holding a doll. Above me, around the russet-coloured walls, hung censers, bronzes and candles, ivory busts, amulets and mosaics. And at my feet surged the white snoods of the female worshippers, from the meanest quarter of Rome—a wave of poverty breaking on the altar steps.

In one of the side chapels, on a little improvised wooden platform, a small girl was delivering a sermon. She could not have been more than eight, with cork-screw curls and a satin dress. She was surrounded by grave, listening grown-ups. She spoke of the Trinity with all the gestures and poses of children who recite something they have learned by heart. It was strange to hear her talking of the sin of Adam, from which our Lord delivered us; of her faith in everlasting life; of the Word become Flesh; of Tertullian and the Latin Church. Having made her speech, she curtsied primly towards the high altar and went off to play with her dolls. Another child replaced her—this time a little boy in a black suit with a white sash across his chest. What would Tertullian have thought had he heard his words on the lips of babes?

The scene in this church struck a Protestant as chaos. For in other parts, other services were going on. I caught snatches of a monkish chant from time to time near the high altar; but the general pandemonium, the universal shouting and singing, drowned any one sound. This was the typical Italian church—with its Corinthian pillars swathed in purple damask; its far-away altar and distant choir. Beneath the canopy of the central altar, the Cardinal and his minions celebrated Mass, surrounded by high wax candles, with those robings and disrobing, the endless putting on and taking off of shoes, sandals, vestments, surplices.

I had seen this Cardinal enter just before, the two fingers of his right hand raised in benediction as the congregation rose and genuflected. What, I wondered as he passed up the aisle, was going on in that mind? Behind those marmorean features of iron will, combined with a sort of tranquil resignation, what was happening? In his face I saw the energy, as well, perhaps, as the monkish rigour, of a man inaccessible, in his unique concern for the greatness of the Church, to human passions.

The worshippers came and went. Artisans and peasants with their wives and children bowed on the steps of the high altar. Old women with baskets holding bottles as well as prayer-books mingled with ladies clad in the latest fashions of the Rue de la Paix—that equality of all classes in church, so notable in Italy. The difference between religious and lay was not great, just as the worshippers did not stop at the doors but extended right out down the steps into the piazza, mingling with the pigeons and souvenir-sellers—who also belonged to the service, in their own Italian way.

After receiving a benediction from a tall monk with a reddish beard which gave him the appearance of some mediæval sorcerer, ·I set out for the Via della Conciliazione, which leads to St. Peter's. It was still early, and here, in this modern boulevard which fronts the Shrine of Christendom, I sat out at a café table, looking towards the great basilica, before which the piazza seemed like some vast ant-heap—tens of thousands of people milling about in an endless coming and going, standing and kneeling, bowing and scraping, awaiting the Papal benediction at midday. On the steps before St. Peter's, Mass was being celebrated at six tables, and around me flocked the Roman and European crowd, to whom the singing of the Vatican choir came over by loud-speakers. In the shaded arcades of Bernini around the oval piazza I passed a priest who sat at a ·table selling indulgences and receiving offerings with an indifference only possible in one long accustomed to accepting money from the poor.

I sat nearby, at the opening of the Via della Conciliazione, listening to the shouts for the waiters, who hurried forward balancing trays with cups of coffee and wine; the bawling of the newspaper-vendors; the clinking of glasses, and the harsh klaxon of the buses that ploughed their way through this crowd, ever adding human fuel to the masses in the square. Who would have thought, in this vast congeries of sound and profane humanity, that this was a great Sunday of Holy Year before St. Peter's—had he not understood something of the Catholic Faith?

At my table a Jugoslav was writing postcards and affixing stamps; at least thirty were going across the Adriatic to his Communist home, to show that, for him at least, the Catholic Faith still existed. At the next table, two German damsels dressed in Girl Guide uniforms, with scurf on their collars from a too hasty toilet, ordered beer with difficulty. There were well-cut suits and dresses that might have come from Schiaparelli's—and ferrety creatures with babies at their breasts who had walked all the way from Naples. There were beggars and tramps; hikers in check shirts speaking Yorkshire; women in cloth breeches with straw hats; children with balloons babbling French. All were here, each making his own noise. Nor were the infirm absent. I saw one poor fellow walking about on his hands and feet like a dog, suffering from that singular Italian disease, *lupomaro*. Like a burthen beneath it all sounded the Mass.

The movement towards the basilica of St. Peter's increased. And as the hour of twelve approached, aeroplanes appeared overhead, circling and dropping pamphlets. I caught one. It was printed in English. *"Buy Cetra Gramophone Records! O Sole Mio will bring Italy and her sun into your home!"* Some landed among the priests officiating at the tables on the steps of St. Peter's; but no one, except some small boys in the piazza, who leapt for them, seemed to take any notice. In the shadow of the Via della Conciliazione it was cool, but the great piazza before the church held like a receptacle the yellow sunshine; and people had made little paper hats out of newspapers.

Just after midday, the windows of the central balcony of St. Peter's opened and a figure in white, his arm upheld, appeared and spoke. And over the loud-speakers came the words the greatest of the Italians used 600 years ago, when he too hoped that European civilisation might still be saved:

"Behold, now is the acceptable time, in which arise signs and consolation and peace. For a new day begins to dawn, that shall dissipate the darkness of long calamity. Now the breezes of the East begin to blow, the lips of Heaven redden, and with serenity comfort the hopes of the people. . . ."

His words continued quietly, almost monotonously for nearly a quarter of an hour in the vast hush that fell. And when he had finished and was withdrawing through the window, his hand still raised as he backed away from us, a deep growl suddenly went up from the silent crowd; it transformed itself into a clamour, and then a cheering, and then a wild huzzaing. From every corner of the piazza went up the cry *"Viva il Papa!"*, echoing down the Via della Conciliazione almost as far as the Castle of Sant' Angelo, and to the Tiber itself. And when I found myself pronouncing these words, if only inaudibly, I felt that the goal I had set myself three months before in Rieti had been reached, and that my Sabine journey was over.

THE END